Competency and the Learning Organization

Donald Shandler, P.h.D

Menlo Park, California

Competency and the Learning Organization
Donald Shandler

CREDITS:
Editor: Mary Kay Beeby, Kay Keppler, George Young
Design and Production: Fifth Street Design, Berkeley, CA

© 2000 Crisp Publications, Inc., Menlo Park, CA 94025

Printed in Canada by Transcontinental Printing

www.crisplearning.com

00 01 02 03   10 9 8 7 6 5 4 3 2

Library of Congress Catalog Card Number 99-75083

Shandler, Donald

Competency and the Learning Organization

ISBN 1-56052-566-5

PART III / IMPLEMENTING SUCCESSFUL COMPETENCY-BASED LEARNING PROGRAMS 61

Implementing a Competency-Based Learning Program 63

PART IV / EVALUATING AND MEASURING COMPETENCY-BASED LEARNING PROGRAMS 81

Evaluation and Measurement 83

APPENDIX 95

Competency
and the
Learning Organization

Introduction

COMPETENCY-BASED LEARNING

···

*Many companies now use competency-based tools and
applications to drive organizational performance.
Competency models influence training and development,
recruiting and staffing, compensation and benefits, leadership and executive development, human resources, and
organizational development initiatives.*

···

For each success story from a leading organization, however, many
other groups struggle to identify competencies and implement
learning programs that will achieve business objectives. Some
companies spend so much time developing competency models that little time or money remains when they are ready to implement their
plans.

This book is designed to guide you through the process. It is organized into four parts: building the foundation, and designing, implementing, and measuring competency-based learning. Discussion is sup-
plemented by practical examples showing how some organizations have
applied the concepts to their programs. If you are an organizational
manager or training professional, you can save yourself and your company or clients time, effort, and money by finding out what competency-based learning is and how other organizations have implemented it
successfully.

Learning Objectives for Competency-Based Learning

The objectives for Competency-Based Learning have been developed to guide you to the core issues covered in this book. When you have finished it, you should be able to:

- define competency-driven learning and performance
- build a foundation for competency-based learning in your organization
- design a competency-based learning program
- implement competency-based programs
- evaluate and measure competency-based programs

Before We Begin: Build a Competency Vocabulary

Much has been written about competencies; consequently, a wide variety of terms and definitions has emerged.

What is a competency?

Competencies have been defined as they relate to work (tasks, results, and outputs) and the characteristics of people doing the work (knowledge, skills, and attitudes). The first step in designing and implementing a competency-based learning program is identifying and publicizing a definition that meets the needs of your organization and its culture. author Scott B. Parry says a competency is:

> ". . . a cluster of related knowledge, skills, and attributes that affects a major part of one's job (a role or responsibility), that correlates with performance on the job, that can be measured against well-accepted standards, and that can be improved through training and development."

What are core competencies?

Core competencies are relevant to the performance of both individuals and organizations. A core competency for the individual is one competency that is essential for the successful performance for a given job at a specific level within the organizational structure. These core competencies change and evolve to meet the needs of the organization. A core competency for the organization is what it does best—the activities that help define the organization's competitive advantage in the economy.

What is the difference between competency-based training and competency-based learning?

These terms are often used interchangeably, but this book uses competency-based learning as the term of preference for true performance improvement.

Competency-based training (CBT) focuses on an individual's immediate job-related needs, often limited to skills acquisition. It is usually a short-term response to an existing problem. Competency-based learning (CBL) focuses on an individual's longer-term, often future job needs. This learning is usually continual and self-directed; in fact, "learning to learn" is one of the building blocks of this process.

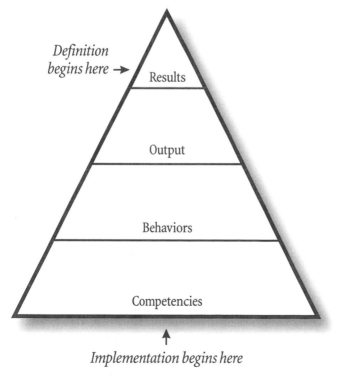

The Competency-Based Performance Pyramid

What is competency-based performance and how does it work?
Competency-based learning results in competency-based performance through the simple and practical application of four steps:

1. Individuals and organizations possess and acquire competencies (knowledge, skills, attitudes).

2. They apply these in the form of behaviors (actions, thoughts, feelings).

3. Their behaviors produce output (products and services).

4. How this is done yields results (performance).

The implementation of CBL begins at the first step with individuals acquiring competencies reflected in behaviors that produce outputs that yield business results. However, the development of a CBL program begins at step four. If you begin with the definition of the desired business results and identify the output and behaviors that produce those results, the competencies that are developed from that data will be the ones that lead you to your desired business results.

SUCCESS STORIES

To help you better understand how you can turn the theory of competency-based learning into reality, five leading organizations will be showcased throughout the book. Their unique implementation of the design, development, and implementation of their systems may give you specific ideas to try in your areas.

EASTMAN KODAK

Through the years, Eastman Kodak has been successful with an abundance of new products and processes that make photography simpler, more useful, and more enjoyable. Today, the company's work increasingly involves digital technology—combining the power and convenience of electronics with the quality of traditional photography to produce systems that bring levels of utility and fun to the taking, "making," and utilization of images.

Kodak has successfully tackled tremendous change during its 100+ years in business. Beyond its obvious technological advances, Kodak realized it also had to be a leader in building a corporate culture that values it employees and their level of satisfaction. In an article written for "The CEO Series," George Fisher, Chairman and CEO, explained his philosophy:

"In these rapidly changing times, it is essential that we give all employees something they can count on, something steadfast and of fundamental importance as the foundation of a renewed culture. At Kodak, we are trying to provide this through our corporate values and principles. I have found that if you continuously stress the sanctity of your key values at all levels of a company, they eventually will take root." Here are Kodak's five key values:

- Respect for Individual Dignity

- Uncompromising Integrity

- Trust

- Credibility

- Continuous Improvement and Personal Renewal

"Why are these values important? They are important because they define who we are and guide how we conduct ourselves with our employees, customers, and shareholders around the world. In fact, they are the essence of our brand. These values and goals must be understood so that everyone works together as one worldwide company. They are our statement that we take seriously our responsibility to be a good worldwide corporate citizen and that we live and do business by these fundamental values. There is no such thing as lip service to these values; we won't tolerate it. In fact, I consider them a condition of employment. Why? Because without values, you have no company."

Employee Training

"Commitment to these values requires that we put them into action in concrete, measurable ways. If we expect our employees to be builders, we must give them the tools and training to build. To grow and maintain a satisfied workforce, Kodak has created a training initiative that gives our employees the most advanced tools available today. As employees become more versatile and 'in demand' in the ever-changing business world, their job satisfaction grows along with the quality of their performance. At Kodak, we call this Continuous Improvement and Personal Renewal—one of our five values.

Under this training initiative, employees work with supervisors to produce development plans to enhance their skills and talents. Every employee receives at least 40 hours of training each year as part of this plan. Our goal is to make our employees more competitive so they can face any new challenge or opportunity. We want our people to be prepared for anything, for if there's one thing that's certain as we approach the 21st century, there's no such thing as lifetime employment anymore —anywhere.

Business leaders and CEOs who focus on the needs of their employees with the same enthusiasm they do for customers and shareowners will create the growth companies of the future," says Fisher.

An important part of Kodak employees' development plans is the identification of competencies required for success. Core competencies were identified at the corporate level and each division adapted these to fit their own business objectives.

The case study in Part III highlights the Kodak Latin American Region's (LAR) unique implementation of their competency-based learning program.

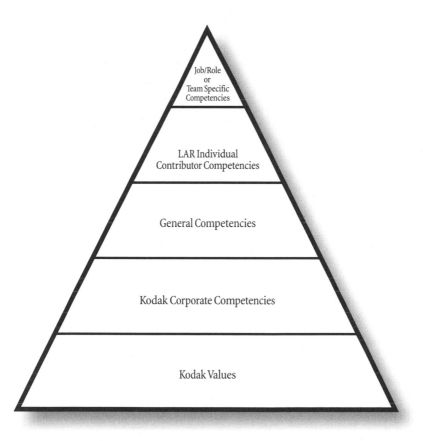

The Kodak Latin American Region (LAR) Model

HON COMPANY

HON Company is the nation's largest manufacturer of value-priced office furniture and fourth largest office furniture manufacturer and marketer in North America. HON Company is also the nation's leading manufacturer and marketer of gas- and wood-burning fireplaces.

C. Maxwell Stanley founded the company in 1945 on the principles of excellence, integrity, and respect for people. From the beginning, he led the company with an inspiration and integrity that enlarged and enriched the lives of all those who worked with him. He chose to call those who worked for the company "members" rather than employees. To demonstrate that they were more than just wage earners, a profit sharing program was established before the firm showed any profit, and he saw to it that additional member benefit and communication programs were developed and implemented far ahead of their time.

The company still pursues a participative environment and culture that nurture the active involvement of each member and attract and retain the most capable people who work safely, are motivated, and are devoted to making the company and themselves jointly prosper.

The HON Company began its competency-based learning model by identifying the business results it expected from each job category: leadership, professional, and individual team member. For each category, the learning team responsible for implementing HON's CBL program identified the knowledge, skills, and attributes members must have to be outstanding performers.

Taking a systems approach, the team achieved buy-in from executive management and then aligned the human resource systems—from hiring through succession planning—to the model. The case study in Part II explains how HON developed an innovative yet cost-effective way to provide learning opportunities based on its core competencies to its supervisors and team leaders without taking them off the job for days at a time.

NATIONAL RETAIL FEDERATION

As the world's largest retail trade association, NRF's mission is to conduct programs and services in research, education, training, information technology, and government affairs to protect and advance the interests of the retail industry. NRF's membership includes the leading department, specialty, independent, discount, and mass merchandise stores in the United States and 50 nations around the world. NRF represents more than 100 state, national, and international trade organizations, which have members in most lines of retailing. NRF also includes in its membership key suppliers of goods and services to the retail industry.

The goal of the NRF's Education Program is to promote retailing as a career at all levels, to promote awareness of the opportunities retail careers offer, and to encourage excellence in retail education by supporting worthy individuals and institutions financially. Although a relatively new function, the education program has gotten off to a strong start.

Working with educators, retailers have developed a comprehensive program of workplace skills and accepted standards to ensure a consistent, trained, and motivated workforce. The NRF Foundation, the NRF's educational branch, works to establish certification programs using these skill standards for retail associates that will decrease the need for company-sponsored training programs. The Foundation's Education Program also promotes retailing as a career and encourages greater understanding of retailing's role in and contribution to the economy. Furthering this goal is a program of scholarships for university and college students pursuing careers in retailing.

The NRF's industry-wide standards are used in Part I as an example of a generic model that can be adapted to any retail environment. Using a generic competency model that is appropriate for your industry or desired business results instead of developing your own from scratch can significantly shorten your design time and save valuable dollars needed in the implementation phase.

SEARS UNIVERSITY

Sears, one of the world's largest retailers, provides a classic example of the rise, fall, and rebirth of a corporate university - and of a major company. In 1992, after almost 100 years in business, Sears realized that a dramatic turnaround was needed to stem the flow of red ink on its balance sheet. Breaking its proud tradition of promoting exclusively from within, Sears brought in a new CEO for the Sears Merchandise Group, Arthur Martinez, from Saks. One of his first tasks was to redefine the workforce. No longer would employees be inwardly focused and seniority-driven. Criteria for hiring and promotion were fundamentally redefined; 12 new leadership competencies, called "dimensions," were established and became the core of what Sears was looking for in both new and incumbent employees.

Those 12 leadership competencies would also be at the core of Sears' new approach to education and training. The new management was committed to converting Sears from "an organization that knew it all" and resisted change to "a learning organization," a term that Martinez has used repeatedly in talking to Wall Street analysts. One of the first steps was to recreate Sears University.

The new Sears University is unlike the old university in many ways. The new university reaches many more employees by redefining training as a "process" rather than an "event." Located at Sears's prairie headquarters outside of Chicago (hence the "Fighting Prairie Dogs" mascot and nickname), the new university increasingly relies on the use of regional training sites and self-paced training and learning. The process is centrally defined and facilitated but, for the most part, controlled and delivered locally.

Sears University is only part of the company's overall approach to training and learning. It partners with trainers and line managers throughout the company providing them with content, advice, and materials. Mark Boyer, the current director, is proud of the classroom training his staff has developed. With a very small staff of internal consultants to produce new courses and select off-the-shelf products, the university works closely with senior executives and line managers to deliver much of the leadership training. "Their use of real-life business cases and the clear demonstration of their commitment to management development are invaluable," says Boyer.

Sears University's self-paced library became the key to extending training and education from 15,000 managers to more than 300,000 associates—and to thousands more employees of other companies that operate specialty retail stores or provide appliance repair and home improvements under the Sears name. Sears's creative use of these materials linked to their core competencies will be showcased in Part II.

MYER GRACE BROS.

Myer Grace Bros., a division of Myer Stores Ltd, is the oldest and largest department store chain in Australia. With more than 70 stores and 27,000 employees, the retailer has multiple outlets in every major metropolitan and suburban area. Within the retailing industry, Myer Grace Bros. is widely respected for its high-quality product lines, as well as for its leading-edge approach to merchandising and customer service.

Bringing that same leading-edge thinking to employee development, the company has invested considerable time and money developing a comprehensive learning and development strategy.

Business Objectives Serve as a Compass

The foundation of Myer Grace's continuous learning program is a model created to help associates understand the key areas of skill and knowledge that will enable the company to achieve its strategic direction. Presented in the form of a compass, this model identifies the principles by which all associates work: trustworthiness, trust, empowerment, and alignment. The four arms of the compass represent the four key areas of skill and knowledge needed for success on an individual and organizational basis.

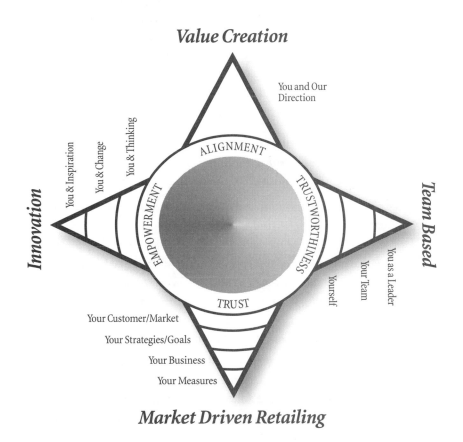

Myer Grace Bros. Continuous Learning Model

In Part II, you will see how Myer Grace Bros. links strategic business objectives to individual development plans. Their implementation process will show how planning and concentrated effort can launch a learning program throughout a vast numbers of locations.

The Learning Organization and Adult Learners

Designing and implementing competency-based learning systems is a win-win-win situation. First, the organization benefits by linking competencies with business strategies. Second, the adult learner profits by the integrated opportunity to learn as part of work. Third, society wins, because CBL is perhaps the boldest strategy for a national vision of continuous learning that responds to workplace change. The bottom line is the same for everyone—developing and maintaining skills required by organizations, individuals, and society for success.

The successful design and implementation of a CBL curriculum is linked to the degree your organization supports learning and the assumptions made about learning.

What is a Learning Organization?

Since the 1990 publication of Peter Senge's *The Fifth Discipline: The Art and Practice of the Learning Organization,* much has been written about the learning organization. This book is based on the belief that:

> *A learning organization views employee learning as an integral part of the work process and a source of competitive advantage and seeks to maximize the benefits of learning by drawing upon the collective wisdom of its workforce. Organizational learning results in a smarter and more competitive system—capable of adapting and leading in an increasingly competitive world.*

Testing Organizational Learning Assumptions

Learning organizations embrace a culture that integrates work and learning. These activities are no longer perceived as separate and distinct activities, but concurrent and synergistic. According to Michael J. Marquardt's *Building the Learning Organization,* these key elements indicate if yours is a learning organization.

- Learning is performance-based and tied to business objectives.
- The organization values learning processes and helping individuals "learn how to learn."
- The ability to define learning needs is as important as the answers.
- The company provides opportunities to develop competency knowledge, skills, and attitudes.
- The organization believes that learning is part of work, a part of everybody's job description.

Development Options For The Learning Organization

Rate your organization on a scale of 1 (rarely) to 5 (always) for the following activities aimed at helping it become a learning organization. My organization strives to:

____ Develop and promote procedures and policies that support learning.

____ Create an environment conducive to learning.

____ Ensure that learning is considered as a continuous resource to improve productivity.

____ Gather data to establish present level of performance.

____ Determine the competency level of learners.

____ Help managers work with employees to meet their developmental needs.

____ Focus learning on activities to change behaviors.

____ Measure progress in learning.

____ Create opportunities for providing feedback.

____ Determine how newly acquired knowledge, skills, and attitudes are applied.

____ Assure a just-in-time menu of quality learning options.

____ Address needs of part-time and remote site workers.

Look at the items you rated 3 or below. What actions can you take to promote these activities in your organization? Think about what actions you could implement in one week, one month, one year.

PART I

Building the
Foundation

A SYSTEMS APPROACH TO ORGANIZATIONAL LEARNING

. . . .

A systems approach to organizational learning is a critical requirement in designing a CBL curriculum, because the CBL curriculum is essentially a system of performance improvement opportunities that develops critical job competencies and enables an organization to achieve its business goals.

A systems approach is an ideal methodology to use to assess organizational needs. Implementation teams who consider key stakeholders throughout any development process have a higher rate of delivering the intended results. A systems approach also enhances organizational learning. It can increase performance by integrating the developmental needs of the employee, manager, and organization.

. . . .

Strategic Learning Systems Model

The use of a systems approach provides a structured mechanism to identify the competency development needs for both the individual and the organization. Systems thinking also establishes general guidelines for critical CBL operations.

The strategic learning systems model serves two purposes. First, it provides an overview of a systems approach to competency-based performance improvement. Second, it reviews the steps that will occur in a successful CBL project. When reviewing the model, prepare to discuss with your CBL project team members questions such as: Where are you in the process? How can you apply this system to your CBL needs? What are your organization's systems strengths? What areas require development?

Step 1. ANALYZE NEEDS

As a first step, determine how critical the need is to the organization's strategic success. What must the company invest in performance improvement to achieve results? In addition, identify return on investment and alternatives to organizationally sponsored performance improvement opportunities.

Step 2. BUILD A COMPETENCY MODEL

Construct one or more competency models to meet the needs of the workforce, emphasizing those competencies necessary for exemplary job performance. Some organizations identify core competencies expected of all employees. Others take the initiative to define specific competencies for each job description. The most complete models define levels of competence within each job category.

Step 3. DESIGN THE CURRICULUM

Develop a comprehensive system of performance improvement, including courses, programs, and learning opportunities linked conceptually. Core curriculums and corporate universities are appearing as innovative responses to this step.

Step 4. IMPLEMENT COMPETENCY-BASED LEARNING

Provide competency-based performance improvement opportunities, ranging from formal group training sessions to informal, self-directed learning experiences.

Step 5. EVALUATE

Monitor the responsiveness of the performance improvement system on two levels: Does it meet the employees' job performance needs? Second, does it meet the strategic needs of the organization?

The following model, used with permission from Dr. David D. Dubois' book, *Competency-Based Performance Improvement: A Strategy for Organizational Change*, visually presents a framework for performance improvement.

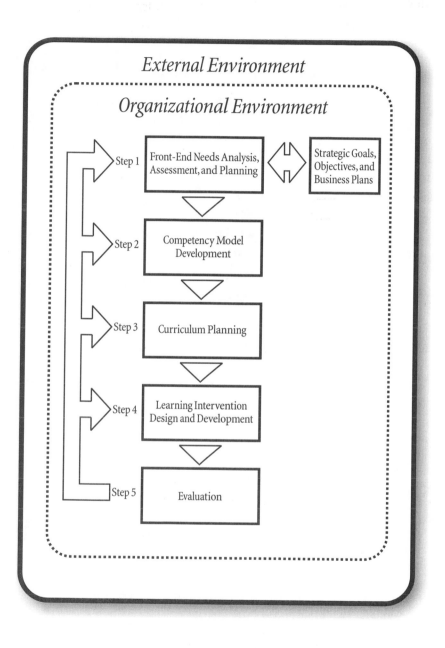

A Framework for Performance Improvement: Adapted from David D. Dubois, Competency-Based Performance Improvement

The Foundation —
Steps 1 and 2

Step 1. ANALYZE YOUR NEEDS

A CBL project team is ideally made up of representatives from key functions of the organization who can identify issues critical to the organization's success. This team must decide what level of investment in performance improvement is warranted, what return on investment can be expected, and what alternatives to company sponsorship are possible.

CBL teams should draw members from throughout the organization. Include employees from the clerical, customer service, manufacturing, professional, technical, salaried, hourly, and management staffs. Upper management must be included to get their future buy-in. These employees have other full-time responsibilities, and persuading them to join another team can be challenging. To get your team off to the right start, clearly identify the purpose of the team and the responsibilities of each member. Develop a plan of action that includes goals and activities for each phase of development. A communication plan to keep key stakeholders, team members, and others throughout the organization informed of progress is critical for success.

Step 2. BUILD A COMPETENCY MODEL

The competency model accomplishes several objectives. First, it identifies core competencies, or key knowledge, skills, and attributes that drive output, results, and quality. Second, once you identify core competencies, you can develop a core curriculum. Finally, it assists you in designing and developing a rich menu of programs that go far beyond traditional instructor-led classroom training.

A competency-based learning model can be designed in several ways. The two suggestions discussed here both have advantages and disadvantages.

Build Your Own Model

If time and resources permit, you may decide to build your own competency model. This method begins with identifying the "what" of the job—what results and outputs are desired and what tasks need to be performed to get those results and outputs. For example, if the desired result for the job of first-line supervisor is to reduce cycle time in production, one action that will contribute to that objective is to retain productive employees.

A. Results	B. Action/Task
Reduce cycle time	• Retain productive employees • Reduce error • Upgrade equipment • ... • ...

The next step is to identify the basic skills for performing this task or action. In this example, a supervisor who gives clear direction, coaches employees, and rewards people appropriately has the basic skills that will contribute to retaining productive employees. This methodology, developed by John Bradford, managing partner of The Bradford Group LLC, recommends going one step beyond to identify outstanding performance. The skills listed in column D are the ones that will result in the model performance for this competency.

What		How	
A. Results	B. Action/Task	C. Basic Competencies	D. Advanced Competencies
Reduce cycle time	• Retain productive employees	• Goal-setting • Coaching • Rewarding employees	• Leading change • Coaching for development • Managing disagreement

This model focuses on both the "what" and the "how" of a first-line supervisor's job responsibilities. It differs from models that begin with defining outstanding performers because it first looks at what you want to achieve before it analyzes how superior performers do it. Thus, if you are successful at developing these competencies, you will be on the right track to accomplish your business objectives.

There are many good methods to build competency models that explain how to define the advanced competencies that result in superior performance. Basically, these methods begin with identifying the criteria for superior performance and then collecting data through behavioral interviewing, 360 feedback, brainstorming sessions with experts, and on-the-job observation. Once the behavioral data is collected, it can be grouped into clusters or patterns to defined competencies. This is where a generic model is particularly helpful. Using generic competency labels and expanded definitions can significantly shorten the development cycle.

It is important to validate the data with surveys of superior and average performers. Performance reviews and selection interviews are two additional opportunities to make sure your model reflects the ideal behaviors. Finally, you may wish to define levels of competency within each category. For example, someone who has basic coaching skills would be able to identify desired performance, seek information, and check for understanding. A superior performer may coach others how to coach effectively.

CASE: *THE HON COMPANY*

The HON Company began its competency-based learning model by identifying the business results it expected from each job category: leadership, professional, and individual team member. For each category, the learning team identified the knowledge, skills, and attributes members must have to be outstanding performers.

Taking a systems approach, the team achieved buy-in from executive management and then aligned the human resource systems—from hiring through succession planning—to the model.

Here is their list of competencies for a supervisor:

Basic Personal Skills

* Applied Learning

* Adaptability/Change

* Planning and Organizing

* Written/Oral Communication

* Delegation/Follow-up

Advanced Leadership Skills

* Team Problem Solving/Decision Making

* Results Achievement

* Teamwork

* Coaching

* Conflict Resolution

The HON Learning Center uses this model as the foundation for its identification and development of learning programs. With an integrated competency model, supervisors can easily select the learning programs for specific competencies they wish to improve.

Customizing Models Designed by Others

If your organization has little time and limited funding to develop its own model, you could alter a model developed by another organization. You can take advantage of the time and research that went into the creation of these models, but you can also customize it for your own company.

Workforce Competency Model

Creating a national vision for continuous learning is a constant challenge for policy makers. Developing an integrated system to train and place workers who have the skills employers need has become imperative for those who have a stake in economic success.

This new, broader, continuous workforce learning initiative has a direct relationship to developing a CBL model. The authors of *Putting Knowledge to Work in the Knowledge Economy* state that "to move the workforce in a new direction, the objective is to identify a number of moving targets: competencies the new work requires, competencies the current work possess, and the gap between the two."

Anthony Carnevale, writing in *America and the New Economy*, lists the 16 skills, or competencies, required of workers in an economy where new, competitive standards are radically changing America's workplace. (Note that many of the competencies that provide a competitive edge are the "soft," nontechnical skills.)

Sixteen Worker Skills Relevant to the New Economy

Learning to Learn
1. Foundation Skills

The Academic Basics
2. Reading Skills
3. Writing Skills
4. Computational Skills

Communication
5. Speaking Skills
6. Listening Skills

Adaptability
7. Problem-Solving Skills
8. Creativity Skills

Development Skills
9. Self-Esteem Skills
10. Motivation and Goal-Setting Skills
11. Personal and Career Development Skills

Group Effectiveness
12. Interpersonal Skills
13. Negotiation Skills
14. Team Work Skills

Influencing Skills
15. Organizational Effectiveness Skills
16. Leadership Skills

Adapted from *America and the New Economy*, Anthony Carnevale. Used with permission.

Workforce Competency Model

In his book, Anthony Carnevale describes two CBL models. In the workforce competency model, each skill is listed. Its importance to the new economy is explained. The curriculum to support the acquisition of the skill is presented. Finally, the question of what constitutes competence in the skill is answered. This example presents a model treatment of one skill.

Leadership Skills: A Model Approach in Building a Competency Model

Overview: Leadership skills in the workplace involve influencing others to serve the strategic purpose of an organization or the developmental needs of the organization.

Importance to the New Economy: The pace of change and the competitive standards in the new economy require workers to assume leadership roles beyond their own formal assignments. Moreover, the new economic environment requires adaptability in leadership roles; every person at every level of an organization may need to assume a leadership role at one time or another, depending on the requirements of the task at hand. In addition, the growing utilization of more flexible technologies and organizational networks are creating more fluid work processes that demand spontaneous leadership.

Curriculum: A curriculum for leadership should do the following:

- Develop an awareness of leadership approaches
- Develop leadership skills, such as personal management, group effectiveness, adaptability, and influencing skills
- Develop leadership behaviors, such as developing and communicating a vision, developing commitment, inspiring effort, and modeling appropriate behaviors

What constitutes competence? At its most elementary level, leadership is the demonstrated ability to influence others to act. Competence is demonstrated by an awareness and application of leadership theories and associated skills and is subjectively assessed by peers, customers, and management.

Office of Personnel Management Model

This second model addresses the competency development needs of individuals and management. It is adapted by Crisp Publications from the Office of Personnel Management of the U.S. federal government. It is particularly valuable if you do not have a list of company-sanctioned business and management competencies, do not know where to begin, or do not have the resources to design your own. The adapted model lists seven skills for individuals and seven for management.

COMPETENCY AND BEHAVIORS

Individual Skills

Communication / (oral, written, listening)

- Expresses ideas and facts in a succinct, organized manner
- Makes clear and convincing oral presentations
- Considers and responds appropriately to ideas expressed by others

Flexibility

- Remains open to change and new ideas
- Adapts behavior and work methods in response to new information, changing conditions, or unexpected obstacles

Conflict management

- Resolves conflicts, confrontations, and disagreement positively and constructively
- Strives for win-win solutions
- Works to minimize negative personal impact

Creativity and innovation

- Develops new insights into situations and applies innovative solutions to make organizational improvements
- Designs and implements needed programs and processes

Customer focus

- Anticipates and meets the needs of clients
- Achieves quality products
- Advocates and takes action for improving services

Process and product improvement

- Assures that internal controls are developed and maintained to ensure the integrity of the organization and its products and services
- Continually improves the quality of products and services

- Identifies simpler, faster, and cheaper processes for achieving highest quality results

Initiative (decisiveness, self-direction)

- Demonstrates belief in own abilities and ideas

- Is self-motivating and results-oriented

- Recognizes own strengths and weaknesses

- Makes sound, well-informed decisions

- Perceives the impact of decisions

- Commits to action to accomplish organizational goals

Management Skills

Managing and developing others

- Ensures that staff is appropriately selected, allocated, appraised, and developed

- Motivates and guides others toward goal accomplishment

- Rewards people for efforts and achievements and ensures that they are treated fairly

- Empowers people by sharing information, knowledge, skills, power, and authority

- Develops lower levels of leadership by pushing authority downward and outward throughout the organization

- Coaches and mentors others

Diversity

- Recognizes the positive influences of diverse cultures, viewpoints, behavioral, and learning styles

- Adapts leadership styles to varying situations

- Builds a workforce that includes and values diversity in race, gender, culture, and other aspects of individual difference

- Leadership (providing vision and direction, fostering commitment)

- Inspires and challenges others

- Takes a long-term view and initiates organizational change for the future
- Builds commitment to the vision with others
- Identifies opportunities to move the organization toward the vision
- Works with others to build vision

Team building

- Manages group processes
- Encourages and facilitates cooperation, pride, trust, and group identity
- Fosters commitment and team spirit
- Works with others to achieve goals

Financial management

- Prepares, justifies, and administers budgets
- Plans, administers, and monitors expenditures to ensure cost-effective support of programs and policies
- Monitors, oversees, and controls revenue-generating activities

Project management

- Determines objectives and strategies
- Develops plans and organizes resources for implementation of projects
- Coordinates with other parts of the organization to accomplish goals
- Monitors and evaluates the progress and outcomes of operational plans
- Anticipates potential threats or opportunities
- Synthesizes large amounts of information into important points

Relational influence

- Considers and responds appropriately to the needs, feelings, and capabilities of others
- Develops networks and coalitions with others who have mutual interests or goals

- Develops networks and coalitions with others who have complementary skills and knowledge

- Gains cooperation from others to obtain and share information and accomplish goals

- Builds consensus and finds mutually acceptable solutions

- Persuades others and influences outcomes

- Develops and maintains awareness of external factors that affect the organization

This model was developed by the Office of Personnel Management and simplified by Crisp Publications to serve as a solid foundation for any organization to adapt to its specific needs.[1]

Retail Professional Competency Model

Unlike leadership skills that apply across industries, competencies for individuals sometimes vary greatly depending on job function. In an effort to identify industry-specific skill standards, the National Retail Federation published its Skills Standards for Retail Professionals in 1998.

Hundreds of retailers, educators, and government representatives participated in the development of skills standards for the retail industry. This was part of a larger effort to define skill standards for all industry segments in conjunction with the National Skills Standards Board.

Skills standards provide workers with a clear definition of what they need to know and do to be successful on the job. The retail skills standards describe the tasks involved for retail sales associates and how professional sales associates should behave in carrying out those tasks. Skills standards also provide a basis for selecting and training a skilled workforce.

The National Retail Federation has developed a certification process based on the skills standards to certify that retail professionals have the necessary skills to be successful on the job. This is a good example of a systems approach to implementing competency-based learning. The project included key stakeholders, involved practitioners and educators, assessed the needs across the entire industry and recommended multiple forms of learning opportunities to provide practical application of the competency-based learning.

[1] Crisp Publications also provides the Competency Builder, a library of 42 self-study courses matched to these competencies.

The following are the six skill categories that comprise the Skills Standards:

Provide Personalized Customer Service

Sell and Promote Products

Monitor Inventory

Maintain Appearance Of Department/Store

Protect Assets

Work As Part of a Department/Store Team

The complete *Skills Standards Model* is presented in the Appendix.

For More Information

Building a strong foundation for a competency-based learning program is essential to its success. The list below is provided to help you learn more about how others have successfully built the foundation for their programs.

Articles

Parry, Scott B. "The Quest for Competencies." *Training*, July, 1996.

Books

Carnevale, Anthony Patrick. *America and the New Economy: How New Competitive Standards Are Radically Changing American Workplaces.* San Francisco: Jossey-Bass Publishers, 1991.

Marquardt, Michael J. *Building the Learning Organization.* New York: McGraw-Hill, 1996.

Meister, Jeanne C. *Corporate Universities: Lessons in Building a World-Class Work Force.* Alexandria, VA: American Society for Training and Development, 1993.

Senge, Peter M. *The Fifth Discipline: The Art and Practice of the Learning Organization.* New York: Doubleday Currency, 1990.

Vicere, Albert A. and Robert M. Fulmer. *Leadership by Design.* Harvard Business School Press: Cambridge: 1998.

Watkins, Karen E. and Victoria Marsick. *Creating the Learning Organization* (In Action Series). American Society for Training and Development: Alexandria, VA: American Society for Training and Development, 1996.

Websites

Eastman Kodak: www.kodak.com

HON Company: www.hon.com

National Retail Federation: www.nrf.com

Sears University: www.sears.com (see section "About Our Company,"

"Careers," "Sears University")

Crisp Publications: CrispLearning.com (see Competency Builder)

PART II

Designing a Competency-Based Curriculum

ASSUMPTIONS ABOUT ADULT LEARNERS

····························

Individuals, organizations, companies, and the press are discussing lifelong learning, the need to "learn new things," and even the mechanics of how individuals impart or acquire knowledge. Fundamental to these discussions— whether from the perspective of educator, trainer, or instructional designer—are the assumptions that we make about adult learners.

····························

Four Classic Assumptions

Malcom Knowles, writing in his now classic book, *The Adult Learner: A Neglected Species* (1984), was one of the first to address the unique needs of adults as learners. Four critical assumptions emerged helping corporate trainers and university continuing educators to better understand their audience. Knowles suggested that:

1. Adults have a need to know why they should learn something.

2. Adults have a deep need to be self-directing.

3. Adults have a greater volume and different quality of experience than youth.

4. Adults become ready to learn when they experience in the life situation a need to know or be able to do in order to perform more effectively and satisfyingly.

An appreciation of these assumptions, and the following discussion, will enhance the design and delivery of effective competency-based learning programs.

Adult Development and Learning Activities

The better we understand the stages of human development, the more effectively we can build learning activities, processes, and systems to enhance it. At each stage of our development, our perceptions shift, providing the learner with the ability to view the world in different ways.

As an example, the new employee may need to focus more on the content of knowledge. A more experienced individual may have learning needs requiring integrating experiences or learning that emphasizes processes. Finally, the highly-experienced learner may have learning needs that emphasizes making connections and linkages that create or reshape context.

The well-worn statement, "One size does not fit all," is most relevant when our attention focuses on adult development and learning activities.

PEDAGOGY AND ANDRAGOGY: IMPLICATIONS FOR THE PRACTIONER

Pedagogy, the art and science of teaching children, has characterized much of our formal "schooling." It makes the assumption that children and youth (and too often adult learners) are primarily motivated by extrinsic motivators of grades, diplomas, parental praise (mom, pop, or the boss). Whereas andragogy, the art and science of teaching adults, suggests that intrinsic motivators (self-esteem, achievement, increased responsibilities, life enrichment) are the more significant drivers of learning for adults.

Malcom Knowles, writing in *The ASTD Training & Development Handbook* (Chapter 12, "Adult Learning") makes the following six recommendations for implementing an andragogical design process.* These recommendations are most relevant to this book and I have taken the liberty of loosely paraphrasing his statements.

- *Climate Setting.* The establishment of a climate for effective learning is a prerequisite for effective learning.

- *Mutual Planning.* People tend to feel committed to a learning activity to the extent that they participated in planning the activity.

- *Learning Needs.* Needs are not determined exclusively by formal assessment processes. A learning need is not a need unless so perceived by the learner.

- *Objectives.* Participants must translate their learning needs into learning objectives—positive statements of directions of growth.

*Used with permission from the publisher.

- *Learning Experiences.* A plan is needed to identify relevant resources for each objective. Broader learning strategies are needed for utilizing these resources.

- *Evaluation.* New ways of evaluation are needed. Increasingly greater emphasis may be placed on finding out what is really happening from the adults learner's perspective and how he or she is performing, not just on-the-job, but in life.

This discussion of adult learner assumptions has suggested the emergence of a "learning facilitator." This unique individual must understand the process of andragogy and its implication for learning.

Meeting the Needs of Adult Learners

The needs of adult learners are well-matched to the process of competency-based learning. Adults bring into a learning situation a background of experience that is a rich resource for many types of learning. This set of experiences provides a broader base on which to attach new knowledge, skills, and attitudes. To appeal to adult learners, the design of CBL must acknowledge this rich experience.

Review these strategies adapted from *Competency-Based Performance Improvement.* Add your own to the list.

CBL strategies that are designed for adult learners need to meet the following criteria.

- They should emphasize the competency, how it relates to achieving job goals, and the role of both the competency and the job goals in achieving organization goals.

- They should involve the learner and make the learner responsible for achievement.

- They should simulate work conditions.

- They should enable employees to see how the learning applies to the job.

Designing a Competency-Based Curriculum

A curriculum is a carefully designed and developed plan for learning, but competency-based learning takes the concept of curriculum a critical next step further, that is, using it as "the platform of choice" for results-driven performance. Unlike training, which is often separated in time, place, and application from workplace performance, CBL is linked to business objectives. The curriculum is one critical component of this system.

Three Approaches to Competency-Based Curriculum

A competency-based curriculum meets the needs of the learning and performance-driven organization in several ways:

- Content specifications for learning are defined in competency terms regardless of format.
- Innovative learning opportunities are provided.
- A framework for linking learning to performance is created.

Integrated Competency-Based Curricula: An Ideal Choice

Designing and implementing competency-based learning is not a hit-or-miss process. Rather, it is a systematic process that integrates learning theory and application. University, government, and business research efforts have identified competency-based concepts and procedures that meet the needs of individuals, teams, and organizations.

An effective application of an integrated competency-based approach to curriculum ensures that individuals have the opportunity to develop critical job competencies at the appropriate level. David D. Dubois, writing in *Competency-Based Performance Improvement,* suggests placing emphasis on both **horizontal** and **vertical** curriculum integration. A horizontal competency curriculum application focuses on the class of jobs within the same level of the organization. A vertical competency curriculum application focuses on jobs that bridge two or more levels of the organization.

BASIC BUILDING BLOCKS

The Mid-America Vocational Curriculum Consortium, Inc. has identified eight sequential steps for planning for competency-based education. Readers are encouraged to obtain their publication, *Competency-Based Education Professional Development Series*, for a detailed discussion of each step.

Designing and implementing competency-based learning requires:

1. Planning for competency-based education

2. Aligning curriculum

3. Managing competency-based education

4. Writing performance objectives

5. Developing teaching/learning strategies

6. Implementing criterion-referenced evaluation

7. Developing components of a unit of instruction

8. Developing learning activity packets

An understanding of these basic building blocks provides the foundation for designing an integrated competency-based curriculum.

INTEGRATED COMPETENCY-BASED CURRICULUM

Traditional training programs have often consisted of a collection of random activities, some presented "just-by-chance" as part of a calendar of events. Additional performance improvement, human resource management, and quality assurance initiatives, led by stakeholders, may concurrently take place in other parts of the organization. It is not surprising that little return on investment or improvement in performance could be measured.

Competency-based performance improvement, firmly rooted to an integrated curriculum, has emerged as the strategy of choice for organizational change. It emphasizes a systems approach to learning and performance that integrates complex factors into a common architecture and designs competency-based learning.

FOUR RECOMMENDATIONS FOR INTEGRATED COMPETENCY-BASED CURRICULUM

Those organizations that build a world-class workforce use competency models that link training to the strategic needs of the business. An organization's ability to identify and respond successfully to new opportunities in the market place is directly related to its ability to develop, maintain, and increase competence—of individuals, teams, and organization. The foundation for this process is an integrated competency-based curriculum. These four actions can help your organization achieve this foundation for increased competency.

Include and develop critical job competencies

To assess job competence, an organization should identify specific tasks, activities, and roles required for exemplary performance; build a job competency model that incorporates these attributes of exemplary performance; and develop methodologies to validate the job competency model.

Select the appropriate level of subject matter

Not all subject matter will suit all adult learners. An integrated curriculum emphasizes organizing specific subject matter, at the appropriate level, for specific jobs. Many organizations stress that learning opportunities for employees should not only address the needs of their present job, but the next level job in the organization. Succession planning has become an extension of the integrated competency-based curriculum.

Emphasize a cross-organizational performance improvement effort

An integrated competency-based curriculum benefits the organization because first, both horizontal and vertical competency acquisitions across all levels of the organization lead to flexibility and responsiveness in the organization. Second, and more broadly, the curriculum can include job orientation, training, on-the-job coaching, performance assessment, and feedback to name a few options.

Enhance worker/learner achievement of the job output with a high quality level

Program design that emphasizes an integrated, competency-based curriculum accomplishes multiple objectives. It defines content and selects and orders learning activities to meet a specific performance need. Effective quality levels are achieved by identifying specific indicators or measures that demonstrate how the learning and performance objective has been achieved. Moreover, learning objectives are stated in terms that the learner will understand, value, and be able to do. Learning and performance become the partners of the competency-based experience.

An integrated, competency-based curriculum emerges as the centerpiece of an organization's business strategy. It provides practitioners and business leaders with a conceptual framework and understandable vocabulary for implementing exemplary practices.

Assessing Your Curriculum

Gap Analysis Overview

Gap analysis is the difference between what happens and what should happen. Some analysts view a performance gap from the perspective of the present and future—the difference between the way things are and the way we want them to be.

Gap analysis may be applied to the performance of an individual worker or an entire workforce. In either case, the competency-based learning challenge is the same. Organizations and individuals need to have better ways of developing and maintaining the competencies required for success. This critical performance gap can be closed by using an integrated, CBL curriculum.

Analyzing the Gap

Let's step back and assess the status of your CBL curriculum. This "curriculum gap analysis" is presented in the format of five questions, followed by recommendations on how to build a CBL curriculum. Review and discuss these questions with your CBL project team. What are your strengths? What areas require further development?

1. Does your curriculum reflect your efforts to move out of "the business of training" and into "the business of learning and performance"?

2. Has your curriculum planning addressed the need for single job-competencies and job goals? Have you translated this into CBL

and performance improvement opportunities?

3. Has your curriculum planning for multiple jobs, or a jobs cluster matrix (see example on next page), been translated into CBL and performance improvement opportunities?

4. Have you developed an organizational-level curriculum plan for all jobs?

5. Have you translated the competency-based curriculum plan into a menu of specific learning and performance opportunities?

Developing a Competency-Based Learning Curriculum: Recommendations

Answering the curriculum gap questions will help you identify your organization's strengths and weaknesses. These recommendations, which parallel the assessment, will help you accelerate the development of this curriculum.

1. To develop a curriculum that helps you move out of the "business of training" and into the "business of learning and performance":

   • Establish innovative educational opportunities beyond traditional instructor-led, classroom-based learning.

   • Eliminate program redundancy through design of a broad-based curriculum.

   • Help the organization succeed with worker-centered learning opportunities.

   • Tailor competency-based learning and performance to the organization's culture and context.

   • Identify cost-effective, time-sensitive CBL opportunities external to the organization.

   • Develop credibility with internal and external clients by using and publicizing a planned, coherent, comprehensive curriculum.

2. To ensure that your curriculum planning addresses the needs for single job competencies and job outputs and that you translate this into CBL and performance improvement opportunities:

   • Examine the relative value and importance of each competency.

   • Use a focus group to analyze the relationships between job competencies and job outputs.

- Employ a competency matrix (previously constructed in the competency model stage) that reflects the realities of the job.

- Identify the relationships between competencies in the curriculum.

- Document the importance of job competencies to the achievement of job outputs.

- Develop a logical, cohesive, and sequential curriculum for the job.

3. To employ a curriculum planning process for multiple jobs or a jobs cluster matrix that translates into competency-based learning and performance improvement opportunities:

- Use a focus group to develop new understandings of jobs, roles, and outputs of work units.

- Use the results of a jobs cluster matrix to analyze the jobs-to-competencies relationship.

- Include a unified and integrated approach to the development of the same or similar competencies for a cluster of jobs across diverse functions of the organization.

- Identify competencies critical for success at all levels of the organization.

- Use a jobs cluster matrix as a communication tool for briefing managers, clients, and project team members.

A *job cluster matrix* identifies similar jobs across diverse functions. Cells contain *job titles* for that function. For example:

	Marketing	*Development*	*Finance*	*Information Systems*
Executives	Sr. V.P.	Sr. V.P.	CFO	CIO
Managing Managers	Sr. Manager	Research Director	Controller	Systems Engineer
First Level Managers	Team Leader	Team Leader	Team Leader	Supervisor

An example of a *jobs-to-competency matrix* follows:

Competency	First Level Managers	Managing Managers	Executives
Integrity	✔	✔	✔
Customer Focus	✔	✔	✔
Strategic Planning		✔	✔
Business Literacy		✔	✔
Global Networking			✔
Developing Associates	✔	✔	
Organizing	✔	✔	✔

4. To develop an organizational-level curriculum plan for all jobs:

   • Create a chart that organizes and presents a core competency development opportunity.

   • Design lower and upper boundary competencies needed for specific jobs.

   • Schedule a menu of competency-development opportunities.

   • Identify and develop core learning opportunities based on one or more core competencies focused at a given level of the organization.

   • Design elective programs that support the acquisition of a core competency.

5. To translate the competency-based curriculum plan into a menu of specific learning and performance opportunities:

   • Recognize that training or education is only one solution to a performance problem.

   • Identify nontraining solutions to correct performance gaps.

   • Develop a continuous information exchange between CBL planning and the organization's goals and objectives.

   • Initiate management briefings to communicate how curriculum plans and learning opportunities translate into performance improvement opportunities.

The decision to design and implement a competency-based learning program reflects the broader commitment to competency-based performance improvement as the strategy of choice for driving organizational change. It also recognizes that competencies, like markets, are not static. A CBL curriculum must be evaluated continually to identify and close the gaps.

Assessing Your Resources to Design Your Own Curriculum

The scope of the curriculum development project is an important element to consider when determining whether to design your own program, partner, or outsource. These 13 questions, from David D. Dubois' excellent book, *Competency-Based Performance Improvement,* can help you determine the scope of a competency-based curriculum planning project. (Questions used with permission of the publisher.)

ASSESS THE SCOPE

Before designing and implementing a CBL curriculum, you need to define the scope of the project and the resources that you have available. How would you answer each of the following questions?

1. Which jobs are subjects of the curriculum analysis and competency development project? How are they related to each other?

2. What delivery systems are available for the proposed curriculum? Are they the most appropriate?

3. What performance improvement opportunities already exist, and how are they related to the present curriculum planning project?

4. How many employees are to be trained or educated, and over what time period? How will they affect the curriculum plan?

5. Where are the employees who are targeted for training or education geographically located? What impact will this have on curriculum planning?

6. What equipment, facilities, staffing, and training technologies are available (or required) for implementing the curriculum plan?

7. What budget and staffing will be available for implementing the curriculum plan?

8. What competency development or acquisition strategies will be adopted for curriculum implementation?

9. Will performance improvement programs be custom developed internally or through contractors? Will off-the-shelf materials be purchased?

10. What extent of coverage and mastery level of the competency model or menu should be included in the curriculum plan?

11. Will pre-intervention competence assessment profiles and individualized training or education plans be used?

12. What competencies must employees have before completing performance improvement opportunities to be included in the curriculum plans?

13. Are the optimal content sequences for the curriculum understood?

Partnering with a Supplier to Design a Curriculum

Designing your own curriculum may not be the best use of your organizational resources. Moreover, doing so may prevent you from providing learning "just in time." Designing a learning curriculum and alternative programs can be a resource-consuming process. Consequently, many organizations decide to partner with a supplier or hire contractors to do the work.

Should you work with a supplier or hire contractors? Ask yourself:

* What options are available?

* What are the benefits of partnering? Of contracting?

* What should you partner? Contract?

* What steps should you follow?

* What are the benefits of using packaged or customized programs?

What options are available?

The organizational opportunities to link business strategies to competency development are many. No one program works for everyone, and you are in the best position to select the best option, or combination of options, for your organization. Consider these:

Internal Development. Continue to make better use of existing resources.

Partnering. Increase capability by melding internal resources with those of a partner who has special expertise.

Contracting. Turn over the entire project to a third party who will assume responsibility for the activity.

Combination of methods. Each CBL project may have different requirements. You may chose to use different options for different projects.

Which choice will you make? Why? What are the unique challenges of your situation that support this decision?

What are the benefits of partnering?

If you want to jump start the design and implementation of the CBL program, your challenge of "doing more with less" clearly points you in the direction of partnering. You are now positioned to enjoy the following benefits.

Strategic readiness. Your organization's changing business strategies, markets, products, and core competencies require responsive learning and performance initiatives. Partnering will accelerate the deployment of these initiatives.

Flexibility. Extending internal resources with partnering capability will increase your flexibility in meeting internal clients' needs without increasing payroll costs.

Competency enhancement. Moving out of the "business of training" and into the "business of learning" requires a broader menu of programs. Self-directed learning and electronic learning technologies can be acquired by partnering.

Enhanced quality. A systems approach to learning requires an integrated curriculum. Traditional training methods have often used materials of uneven quality. However, employees have come to expect cohesive and well-planned learning materials, which often can be better supplied through the resources of a partner.

Other partnering advantages include expanded capabilities, larger or repositioned staff responsibilities, unit cost reduction, new perspectives, and refocused time and energy of management staff.

How Do I Know What to Partner?

Just as companies focus on their core competencies, returning to what they do best, successful education and training organizations are looking at how they can be most effective. To help you decide how you can maximize your impact, think about the activities that your organization performs.

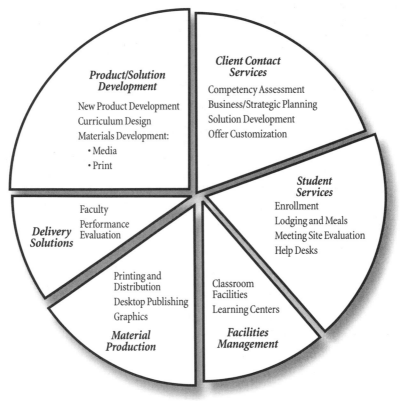

This illustration, based on one appearing in "Outsourcing in Training and Education," presents the functions and services required in support of training, and learning and performance initiatives. In many cases, the work required by some functions prevents you from using your time well. This is where the advantage of partners emerges.

Determine which of these activities is most critical to the business. Is it strategically important? Mission critical? Can the business survive without it?

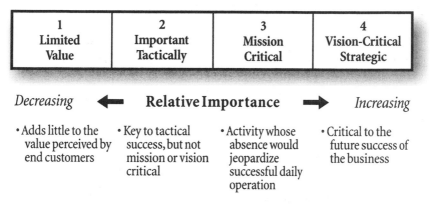

1 Limited Value	2 Important Tactically	3 Mission Critical	4 Vision-Critical Strategic

Decreasing ← **Relative Importance** → *Increasing*

• Adds little to the value perceived by end customers	• Key to tactical success, but not mission or vision critical	• Activity whose absence would jeopardize successful daily operation	• Critical to the future success of the business

Finally, consider capability costs by using the following scale:

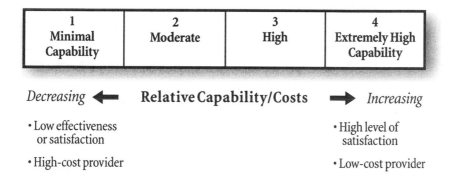

1 Minimal Capability	2 Moderate	3 High	4 Extremely High Capability

Decreasing ← **Relative Capability/Costs** → *Increasing*

• Low effectiveness or satisfaction	• High level of satisfaction
• High-cost provider	• Low-cost provider

Evaluation Exercise

Check the services that apply to you. Rate each activity's importance and your internal capability to deliver. A value of 1 is low; a value of 4 is high. Considering relative importance and relative capability, determine which services you should keep in-house, which you should find a partner to work with, and which you should contract to a third party.

Function	Service	Importance 1 - 4	Capability 1 - 4	Keep Inside (I) Partner (P) Outsource (O)
Client Contact	Competency Assessment Business/Strategic Planning Solution Development Customizing			
Student Services	Enrollment Lodging and Meals Meeting Site Evaluation Help Desk			
Facilities Management	Classroom Facilities Learning Center			
Materials Production	Printing and Distribution Desktop Publishing			
Delivery Solution	Faculty Performance Evaluation			
Product/Solution Development	New Product Development Curriculum Design Materials Development			

Your answers may suggest that you should retain the functions of Client Contact and Delivery Solution, partner on Product/Solution Development and Material Production, and let go of Student Services and Facilities Management. However, no answers are "correct." You must decide what is best for your organization.

With Whom Should I Partner?

Designing and implementing a successful competency-based learning program is a high visibility activity with far-ranging consequences. Here are some questions to consider in selecting a partner to design and implement a CBL curriculum.

Does the partner have a proven track record in creating similar curricula in other organizations?

Is there evidence of creativity and resourcefulness in responding to changing client requirements? Does the partner adapt to your resources and constraints?

Does the partner have the managerial and professional talent to support all phases of product/solution development and materials production?

Has the partner demonstrated business and management acumen?

Has the partner demonstrated best-in-class performance? How are they positioned in the marketplace? What do clients, competitors, and peers think of them?

Rating Form

A rating form, commonly used in problem-solving activities to select from multiple alternatives, can help you determine the best partnering option. Used as a group tool, it will help you clarify common criteria and agree on your eventual selection.

Begin by listing your criteria in the first column. Then assign a relative weight to each one. The total weight for all criteria should equal 100%. For example:

Criteria	Weight	Partner 1	Partner 2	Partner 3
Breadth of content	30%			
Low cost	30%			
Technology solutions	10%			
Competence of designers	30%			
Total	100%			

Next, rate each potential partner on a scale of 1 (low) to 10 (high) for each criteria.

Criteria	Weight	Partner 1	Partner 2	Partner 3
Breadth of content	30%	3	9	5
Low cost	30%	5	8	1
Technology solutions	10%	9	5	8
Competence of designers	30%	7	6	9

To total the scores, multiply the rating in each category times the weight factor. Then add the scores in each column.

Criteria	Weight	Partner 1	Partner 2	Partner 3
Breadth of content	30%	3 x .3 = .9	9 x .3 = 2.7	5 x .3 = 1.5
Low cost	30%	5 x .3 = 1.5	8 x .3 = 2.4	1 x .3 = .3
Technology solutions	10%	9 x .1 = .9	5 x .1 = .5	8 x .1 = .8
Competence of designers	30%	7 x .3 = 2.1	6 x .3 = 1.8	9 x .3 = 2.7
Total	100%	5.4	7.4	5.3

If you and your team have done a thorough job of identifying the criteria and assigning relative importance, the clear winner here should be Partner 2.

How Can You Use Off-the-Shelf or Customized Programs?

A CBL program is judged ultimately by its performance. The bottom line is the linking of competencies to business goals. Achieving these results in a timely, cost-effective, and quality manner is an important component of this process.

Under ideal circumstances, where resources of time, money, and staff may not be an issue, designing the entire CBL program from scratch would be a most attractive option. However, even when infinite resources are available, this may not be the best solution. Since business strategies and core competencies change continually such "designing from scratch" initiatives may be out-of-date by the time the ink is dry. "Just too late" is more often heard than "just in time."

OFF-THE-SHELF CBL MATERIALS

A wide variety of excellent, competency-based, group, and self-directed learning resources are available to meet your organization's performance improvement needs.

There is no reason that an off-the-shelf program cannot meet the same standards that you would develop for your own program, because off-the-shelf materials must pass the same criteria used for sound instructional design and development, and they must address the needs of the adult learner. These requirements for CBL materials include practical ideas and examples to reinforce key concepts, easy-to-follow format, real world case studies, exercises and self-evaluations, and assessments.

As you evaluate your options, the final test is the same for all CBL programs. Three important questions must be answered: Does the program enable people to learn what it was designed to teach? Does it enable them to use on the job what they have learned? Does their education help the organization achieve business results?

Customized Off-the-Shelf CBL Programs

You can enhance off-the-shelf CBL programs cost effectively by customizing them. As Bob Filipczak, senior editor of *Training Magazine* says, "Who can resist the temptation, without reinventing the wheel, to adjust the spokes a little?" Consider his recommendations for customizing.

Adjust the Spokes

Organizations find that modest customization of off-the-shelf courseware meets their learning and performance needs, including corporate cases to enhance a well-designed published program.

Team Up with a Supplier

Finding and establishing a relationship with the right supplier can save time. Often the supplier can modify the program and do the customization faster, better, and more cost effectively than you could.

Exercise Your Options

Customization can range from changing workbook logos and illustrations to a cover-to-cover tailoring process. You may find that different approaches are better for different CBL programs.

Customize for the Individual

In some cases, customization on an individual basis is desirable. The concept of job competencies suggests that learners are in the best position to decide what is relevant in their work area. Creative instructional design techniques are required to make this approach cost-effective.

Incorporate Action Learning

Action learning, which brings real problems into the classroom, provides participants with the opportunity to work on real problems and situations, which also increases the potential for direct transfer of learning.

Respect Copyright and Intellectual Property Rights

Avoid altering and reproducing packaged programs without the knowledge, involvement, and written approval of the publisher. It is unprofessional and illegal.

CASE: *THE HON COMPANY "ADJUSTS THE SPOKES"*

The HON Company Learning Center launched its new supervisory certification program after an extensive competency model development process. HON's list of supervisory competencies appears on page 29.

With multiple locations and a busy management staff, they were looking for self-paced, practical learning materials that fit within their recently reduced training budget. The CBL team found a supplier with many self-study courses that applied to their learning model. From a list of 200, they selected 10 courses matched with videos that supported their supervisory competencies.

Adding custom covers and six pages at the front of each book linked each course back to the vision for learning at HON. Placing assessments at the back of each book allowed the Learning Center to determine if their supervisors were gaining the knowledge. The Center launched the program by sending a catalog to all supervisors. The course supplier administers the entire program, saving key HON resources for more critical tasks.

When supervisors place an order, they receive a book and instructions to check out the video from their local learning center. Their manager is notified of the course objectives and encouraged to initiate a learning discussion with the supervisor. When the participant returns the completed assessment, it is graded and a certificate sent to the manager to be awarded to the participant. Along with the certificate, managers receive a memo with specific discussion questions and coaching suggestions to reinforce the new behaviors back on the job.

Selecting Delivery Options

For those who think that a single product or set of materials will solve their learning and performance needs, let me say, this will not work for CBL. Each performance improvement initiative should be considered as a time-limited project requiring its own set of learning opportunities.

Each organization has its own culture, which is influenced by the products and services it provides. Corporate culture can influence the selection of a CBL delivery option by placing greater emphasis on group or self-directed learning; by requiring learning to occur at many sites for many individuals; and by restricting participant time, equipment, facilities, or instructors. Your effectiveness will be increased if you:

- Study the characteristics of those adult learners and the targeted CBL and performance initiative. What observations can you make about their work environment, competency level, and preferences on how they learn?

- Ensure that the competencies targeted for improvement are addressed in the delivery option.

- Assess how information is taught. This includes instructional methods of lectures, games, demonstrations, case studies, group discussion, exercises, role-plays, and simulations.

- Evaluate how information is presented, including computer-based training, multimedia, interactive TV, electronic text, teleconferencing, groupware, audio and video, electronic performance support systems, online help, even virtual reality.

- Consider how information is distributed, including satellite and cable TV, the Web, or computer disks or networks.

- Conduct a cost-benefits analysis of delivery options. This includes evaluating cost-effectiveness, quality of instruction, and group vs. self-paced learning.

- Consider what delivery options best address learning and performance trends, including rapid deployment of training, delivering training to meet specific needs, teamwork training, measuring performance outcomes, and virtual organizations.

Competency-Based Learning Delivery Options

CBL delivery options can be classified in several ways, although the boundaries are not firmly drawn and several options could fall into more than one category. For example, a video can be used for both group and self-directed learning, and distance learning is an example of both group and technology-driven learning. Three categories are discussed here.

1. Learning with Others

Many socially interactive learning options exist in this category. These range from classroom settings to less formal and workplace settings. This people-intensive approach to learning strengthens the process of organizational transformation and performance by meeting the social and behavioral needs of learners.

A listing of options included in the category of "learning with others" includes case studies, job rotation, clinics/laboratories, on-the-job training, community service, mentoring, courses, role-plays, discussion groups, seminars, games and simulations, and workshops.

2. Self-Directed Learning

This basic principle of the learning organization can take the form of reading and self-study; in its newest and high tech form, it may be a multimedia program. Self-directed learning can usually occur anytime, anywhere.

A listing of options included in this category of "self-directed learning" includes self-assessment/self-testing materials, contract-based learning, books, audio tapes, video tapes, correspondence courses, home study programs, job aids, projects/assignments, and directed readings.

3. Technology-Driven Learning Options

"Emerging technologies" such as digital electronics, optical data storage, and distributed computing (Internet/intranet) are expanding the potential of the personal computer and telecommunication services. These new "technological multipliers" can improve quality, increase productivity, and expand the availability of competency-based learning and performance options.

The personal computer, a critical ally of training, has emerged as the centerpiece of the technology-driven organization. Self-directed, interactive, electronic systems now deliver relevant learning at teachable moments.

Options included in this category of "technology-driven learning" include multimedia, CD-ROM, teleconferencing, distance learning, video conferencing, electronic performance support systems, one- and two-way video, and Internet/intranet.

Developing the Right Mix For You

Each organization's response to designing a competency-based learning program is targeted to meeting its business goals and performance improvement needs. The planned, structured approach that provides employees with an opportunity to acquire competence can range from cost-effective use of group training programs to the flexible and time-sensitive application of self-study resources to sophisticated CD-ROM multimedia learning programs. Usually organizations "mix and match" off-the-shelf and customized resources both to boost performance and productivity and meet participant learning styles.

CASE: *SEARS UNIVERSITY CORRESPONDENCE PROGRAM*

A key component in Sears's recent dramatic comeback as one of the world's largest and most enduring retailers is CEO Arthur Martinez's focus on the basics. When he took over the leadership of the company in 1995, he outlined three key objectives. Sears was to become a compelling place to shop, a compelling place to work, and a compelling place to invest. To support the second initiative, Sears University was restructured to focus on 12 core leadership competencies.

With an employee base of more than 300,000, Sears faced a major challenge to find a cost- and time-effective way to offer competency-based learning to its employees. An integrated approach through the University provides learning opportunities in the form of in-classroom training in regional centers, on-the-job mentoring, in-store presentations, audio tapes, video tapes, highly customized CDI video-based programs, and an extensive correspondence program available to all associates.

Although Sears had offered a correspondence program since the 1950s, participation had been declining. The complexity and inconsistency of materials discouraged active participation. Linkage of the program to associate career advancement was unclear and certification programs were not offered for all courses. To reenergize the program and make it part of the integrated approach to learning, Sears University selected a supplier that matched 19 courses to its 12 competencies. Course materials were easy to use, consistent, and testable.

Success of the correspondence program has encouraged Sears to expand the number of titles each year. In 1999 the company offered 54 basic, intermediate, and specialty courses. The supplier administers the entire program, processing orders, shipping courses, summarizing monthly activity, and awarding certificates, keeping Sears administrative costs to a minimum.

A "check" placed in the grid box indicates that the Transformational Leadership dimension listed across the top is addressed in the course listed below.

	Change Leadership	Integrity	Customer Service Orientation	Empowerment	Interpersonal Skills	Team Skills	Two-Way Communication Skills	Valuing Diversity	Developing Assoc. & Valuing Their Ideas	Business Knowledge/Literacy	Problem Solving Skills	Initiative/Sense of Urgency
BASIC TRAINING												
#101 Customer Satisfaction		✓	✓		✓							✓
#102 Telephone Courtesy and Customer Service			✓									
#103 Professional Selling		✓	✓									
#111 Quality Customer Service			✓				✓					
#112 Calming Upset Customers			✓		✓		✓				✓	
#113 Closing: A Process Not a Problem			✓				✓			✓		
ADVANCED TRAINING												
#201 The Business of Listening			✓		✓		✓	✓				
#202 Better Business Writing							✓					
#203 Effective Presentation Skills							✓					
#211 Developing Positive Assertiveness					✓		✓					
#212 Thinking On Your Feet					✓		✓					
#213 Art Of Communicating					✓		✓					
#301 Stress That Motivates	✓											
#302 12 Steps to Self Improvement		✓			✓	✓	✓					
#303 Personal Time Management											✓	
#311 Attitude: Your Most Priceless Possession			✓		✓		✓				✓	✓
#312 Self-Empowerment	✓			✓								✓
#313 Achieving Job Satisfaction				✓								✓
#401 Basic Business Math										✓		
#402 Understanding Financial Statements										✓		✓
#403 Managing Change At Work	✓					✓				✓		
#411 Creativity in Business	✓			✓						✓	✓	✓
#412 Mentoring	✓			✓	✓		✓	✓	✓			
#413 Ethics in Business		✓								✓		

For More Information

Designing a competency-based curriculum that meets your business objectives is a challenging task. The list below is provided to help you learn more about how others have designed their programs.

Articles and Booklets

Knowles, Malcom S. *The ASTD Training & Development Handbook* (Chapter 12, "Adult Learning")

Crisp Editors, *Extending the Corporate University,* Crisp Publications, Menlo Park, CA: 1997.

Competency-Based Education (Volume 8): Professional Development Series. Stillwater, OK: Mid-America Vocational Curriculum Consortium, Inc., 1992.

Books

Dubois, David D. *Competency-Based Performance Improvement: A Strategy for Organizational Change.* Amherst, MA: Human Resources Development Press, 1993.

Harrison, Nigel. *How to Design Self-Directed and Distance Learning Programs.* New York: McGraw-Hill, 1998.

Knowles, Malcom S. *The Adult Learner: A Neglected Species.* Np: Publishing company, 1984.

Knowles, Malcom S. *Designs for Adult Learning.* Alexandria, VA: American Society for Training and Development, 1995.

Overfield, Karen. *Developing and Managing Organizational Learning: A Guide to Effective Training Project Management.* Alexandria, VA: American Society for Training and Development, 1998.

Piskurich, George M. and Ethan S. Sanders. *ASTD Models for Learning Technologies: Roles, Competencies and Outputs.* Alexandria, VA: American Society for Training and Development, 1998.

Spencer, Lyle. *Competence at Work: Models for Superior Performance.* New York: John Wiley & Sons, 1993.

Maul, June Paradise and Krauss, Joel D. "Outsourcing in Training and Education" in *The ASTD Training & Development Handbook: A Guide to Human Resource Development* by Craig, Ed and Robert L. New York: McGraw-Hill, 1996. Pp. 1008-1030.

PART III

Implementing Successful Competency-Based Learning Programs

IMPLEMENTING A COMPETENCY-BASED LEARNING PROGRAM

· ·

Implementing a successful competency-based learning program is not done accidentally. Ideally, if you have chosen to use a systems approach, you will find that your CBL initiatives become self-marketing. This momentum will continue if you clarify the roles and responsibilities of critical CBL stakeholders and address the implementation requirements for your delivery options.

· ·

Clarifying the roles of stakeholders requires that you assume responsibility as a member of the CBL project team, identify senior managers who can provide organizational support, encourage supervisors to support the CBL needs of employees, and encourage individual learners to assume responsibility for their own learning and performance. As you accelerate efforts at implementation, you must involve CBL stakeholders in addressing the unique requirements for each delivery option: learning with others, self-directed learning, and technology-driven learning.

Role of the Project Team

Implementing a CBL program can be challenging for two reasons. First, it usually implies that you have designed and developed a core curriculum that consists of a wide variety of learning opportunities. Secondly, this curriculum will usually incorporate learning methods that go well beyond instructor-led, classroom-based training programs.

A visit to a typical learning organization will reflect concurrent activities of group instruction, self-directed learning, structured on-the-job learning, and technology-delivered learning options. The good news: the learning organization appears to be learning. The bad news: It may not have the appropriate policies and procedures to support this multidimensional, continuous learning process. The project team plays a critical role in insuring the success of the learning initiatives.

Sustain a Relationship within Stakeholders and Sponsors

Competency-based learning programs are high-visibility performance improvement initiatives that go well beyond a traditional training course. Your project team has spent considerable time and effort in designing strategies to enhance performance. Implementation effectiveness can be increased if you continue your efforts to sustain high visibility and support of stakeholders and sponsors. Here are three suggestions:

1. Maintain communication with all internal and external stakeholders involved in the design and development of each CBL project.

2. Secure public support from senior management, sponsors, and stakeholders who can add legitimacy to the program.

3. Identify informal opinion leaders who are influential within the specific CBL target group. Involve them early in pilot programs to test the learning program. Enlist their support in communicating the benefits of the program to their peers.

The traditional training department that has shifted its emphasis to learning and performance must now cultivate and gain support of its expanded internal/external stakeholders, sponsors, and customers.

Develop a Communication and Marketing Plan

The implementation of a successful CBL program builds on cultivating sponsors and stakeholders to focus on developing communication and marketing plans. This requires a consistent project team effort using multiple communication channels including executive briefings, work group meetings, and announcements.

Communication Strategies

Communication Strategy One: Keep the Big Picture in Focus for Stakeholders

Implementation teams involved in activity-intensive training tasks sometimes lose sight of the bigger picture for themselves and their internal clients. Any CBL performance improvement initiative requires the CBL project team to keep all stakeholders and sponsors informed in every stage of implementation. Communicate the background of the

CBL initiative, what the performance objectives are and how they will be achieved, and bottom-line projections. Don't forget to keep management involved and appraised of progress.

Communication Strategy Two: Use Status Reports for Implementation Updates

Effective communication, like performance, is continuous. Efforts at keeping stakeholders aware of the implementation of the CBL program must be supported by the continuous communication activities of the CBL project team. Far too often CBL implementation fails, not because of program quality, but because stakeholders don't know what's going on.

You can share the responsibilities of communicating by determining what information should be communicated, identifying who should communicate it, and selecting how and when this will be communicated. Follow a carefully developed plan and build credibility by staying on schedule. If your stakeholders are informed, your program has a better chance of succeeding.

Guidelines for Implementing the CBL Program

Implementing a CBL program requires the continuous support of the learning organization, because it is an integral extension of the organization's business strategies, culture, and activities. The following guidelines help you identify and adapt general principles that would support the implementation of a CBL program. The guidelines are based on material appearing in *Building the Learning Organization* by Michael Marquardt. After the example provided, state your own example of how your organization supports the implementing of competency-based learning.

GUIDELINES FOR IMPLEMENTING THE CBL PROGRAM

1. Align organizational learning with business and personal success.

Example: Design pre-learning, learning-event, and post-learning activities that are integrated into key business strategies.

Your example:

2. Build learning into all operations and activities.

Example: A car development learning laboratory that uses a computer simulator and related tools to aid systems engineering, and a coffee pot and comfortable chairs to enhance reflection and conversation.

Your example:

3. Recognize and reward learning.

Example: People who collect and transfer knowledge from internal or external sources are commended.

Your example:

4. Generate many learning opportunities.

Example: Learning forums are designed with explicit learning goals in mind.

Your example:

5. Set aside time for learning.

Example: Only if top management explicitly frees up employees' time for this purpose does learning occur with any frequency.

Your example:

6. Create a physical environment and space for learning.

Example: Designate and equip learning resources centers at each corporate location.

Your example:

7. Maximize learning on the job.

Example: A large consulting firm has developed a continuous work-place learning model that attempts to capture as much on-the-job learning as possible.

Your example:

The Critical Role of the Supervisor

Successful implementation of competency-based learning programs is the result of a partnership. The CBL project team, senior management, and stakeholders can assume a leadership role in the design of a CBL program, but unless the supervisor supports the initiative, the results will be disappointing. Five critical contributions that the supervisor can make include:

1. Help the employee align learning and performance goals with business goals.

2. Discuss learning and performance expectations before, during, and after the CBL event.

3. Provide learners with adequate time during the workday to complete self-directed and group learning programs.

4. Use structured on-the-job methods of coaching and mentoring to support learning and performance initiatives.

5. Assist the employee in integrating what they learn into workplace, performance-driven applications.

CASE: *KODAK LATIN AMERICAN REGION*

The role of the supervisor is key to providing 40 hours of training per year to Kodak's 6,200 employees across Latin America. The region's supervisors guide and instruct members of their work groups through the *Performance Excellence* program. The supervisor-as-trainer approach enables each supervisor to act as a coach and mentor. It encourages the application of learning directly to work situations and promotes teamwork among members of each work group.

LAR's 1997 Performance Excellence course materials included 10 workbooks in Spanish, Portuguese, and English, packaged in a box for each participant, and a supervisor's guide for each team leader. Each two-hour program is simple, interactive, and applicable to a variety of work situations. Supervisor guides contain step-by-step instructions that enable even non-trainers to succeed.

Responsibility for Learning

Adult learners must be encouraged to take responsibility for their own professional growth, learning, and performance. "Learning to learn" is a critical new workforce competency, and CBL can put this concept into action. Moreover, employees must take a leadership role in using what they learned on the job. The adult learner must view learning as an integral part of the work process and a source of competitive advantage.

CASE: *BANK OF MONTREAL*

When the Bank of Montreal decided to shift its culture to a learning organization, it dedicated time and resources to creating its Corporate University Institute of Learning. As part of the launch of the university, the bank wanted employees to understand their role in their own development and be motivated to embrace learning.

The bank used a guide to learning workbook to market the Institute and prepare trainees for a positive experience. The off-the-shelf workbook was customized by replacing the existing case studies with banking-related examples and provided in both French and English versions.

A workbook was sent to each participant before attending training classes at the Institute. The easy-to-use format reduced anxiety and helped trainees look forward to a positive learning environment. A short assessment let them identify their own learning style and consider techniques to use during the class.

The workbook was so successful that once the training was completed, participants took copies of it back to their business units and worked with associates to increase their understanding of individual learning styles. Attendees in effect became advocates of the Institute for Learning.

Implementation Requirements for Delivery Options

CBL delivery options include Learning with Others, Self-Directed Learning, and Technology-Driven Learning. Sometimes the boundaries of these delivery options can blur, but each delivery option may require a different implementation strategy.

Self-Directed Learning

Self-directed learning (SDL) media formats range from paper and pencil to multimedia. In some organizations the SDL experience occurs in the immediate work area, and in others it may take place in a formal learning center. Greater opportunities for telecommuting now allow the learning to take place at home. In each case, the SDL alternative must consider the needs of management, supervisor, and learner.

Management's SDL implementation needs

The CBL team should brief executives with actual materials, explaining how the learning process works and encouraging managers to experience it themselves. In some organizations this is a requirement. Explain how they can support the administration of the program and the learning itself. Demonstrate the relationship of this particular CBL product/process to the broader CBL curriculum. Managers will be more interested in supporting these programs if they see the direct linkage to their business goals.

Supervisor's SDL implementation needs

The supervisor becomes part of the learning support team effort and can enhance the SDL program's implementation. Encourage supervisors to motivate and guide learners.

Learner's SDL implementation needs

Four steps are recommended for employees who use SDL resources. First, prospective learners should be introduced to the competency of "learning to learn" and shown how it will benefit them directly. Second, the advantages and disadvantages of this delivery option are presented. Third, employees should understand the mechanics of the learning package and implementation. Fourth, reinforcement and support for using the new system and fielding general questions should take place.

Self-Directed Learning Implementation

CASE: *MYER GRACE BROS.*

To initiate its corporate-wide learning and development strategy, Myer Grace Bros. invested considerable time and money developing a comprehensive launch plan. The company sponsored formal launch events in each of its regions to ensure that all associates understood the following:

- How the learning program supported Myer Grace Bros. business objectives

- The individual's responsibility to develop skills

- The mechanics of the learning program

- Support for implementing learning plans

Before the orientation program was presented to the entire company, a pilot launch was held in the Queensland region. Feedback interviews from participants evaluated the launch meeting, ordering system, personal progress passport that serves as the individual's learning plan, and the assessment process. The launch program was refined and then implemented throughout the country.

During the launch meeting, participants were encouraged to create an individual development plan to support continuous learning, a cornerstone to the success of the program.

The positive responses from associates created a celebratory atmosphere at the launch. Skits and costumes helped make the program seem friendly and accessible to everyone.

The flowchart on the following page illustrates how continuous learning is linked to business objectives and individual development plans.

Learning Steps   Tools to Assist

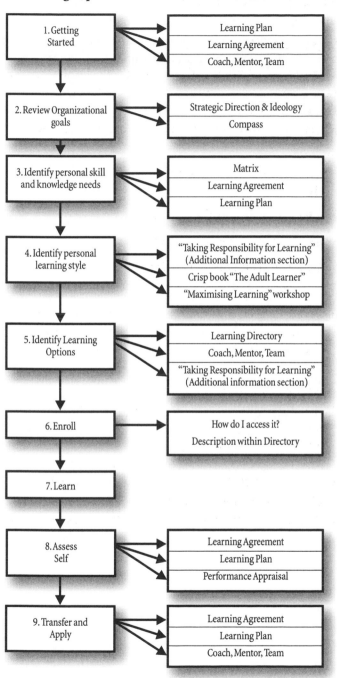

Myer Grace Bros. Learning Process

The individual learning plan

The tool used to translate business objectives into learning opportunities for the individual is the learning plan. Associates work through each section to understand how best to implement their plans.

Individual learning plans include:

• Preferred learning methods

• Personal goals

• Skill assessments

• Learning needs identification

• A learning contract

• A feedback diary

• An application plan

Using the learning directory, which describes learning opportunities, associates design their custom development plans and document them in the learning contract. Supervisors, mentors, and team members act as coaches. High involvement of everyone in the organization reinforces the importance of continuous learning.

A Learning Opportunity Matrix from the Myer Grace Bros. Learning Directory appears on the next page. Participants use this to easily identify appropriate courses to support their competency development.

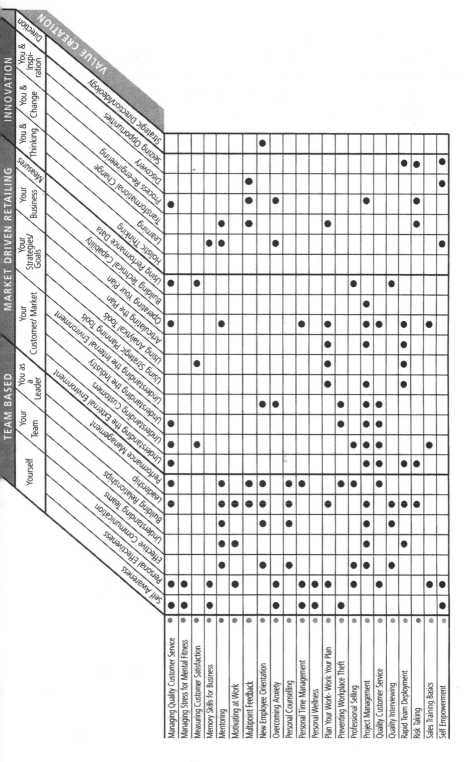

Learning in Groups

Instructor-led, classroom-based group learning activities—workshops, seminars, and courses—continue to have a place in the learning organization. Their effectiveness is heightened when they include selective electronic learning strategies. Use the following guidelines.

Recommendations for implementing group learning activities.

- Reaffirm the relationship of your program to those competencies that support your organization's goals and business plan.

- Focus on job competencies and the achievement of critical job outputs.

- Design a group learning strategy that operates at minimal cost and delivers learning that can be applied.

- Demonstrate organizational support for group learning:

- Develop policies that communicate about the value and importance of CBL and your organization's commitment to training, educating, and developing people.

- Communicate why group learning is required, who's involved, the resources required, and how, when, and where it is carried out.

- Make an effort to reduce ambiguities about the nature of the learning.

Checklist: Implementing CBL Through Group Learning

Demonstrate support of the managers for implementing group learning by helping them to:

- Understand their responsibility to support group learning by reducing work-related conflicts and creating time to learn.

- Express a willingness to be involved before, during, and after the group learning as facilitator, mentor, coach, and team member.

Demonstrate support for the individual learner attending the group learning by:

- Preparing the learner for each group learning experience before the event and following up after it.

- Developing an understanding of the relationship between on-the-job and off-the-job learning.

Technology-Driven Learning

Electronic media have created almost limitless possibilities for heightened learning, and competency-based learning programs can be enhanced by "just-in-time," "just-what's-needed," and "just-where-it's-needed" electronic transfer of knowledge and skills. The implementation of technology-driven learning (TDL) options require that a distinction be made between instructional methods, or how information is taught to learners; presentational methods, or how information is presented to learners; and distribution methods, or how information is delivered to learners. Moreover, implementing TDL requires the support of managers, supervisors, and learners. This "partnership in implementation" is one of the most critical components of CBL programs.

Managers, TDL implementation needs

The leadership and support of senior management is needed to implement TDL options. First, managers must communicate a vision that links improvement initiatives with continuous learning through technologies. Second, managers must make available appropriate TDL options, including self-paced courseware and group learning video-teleconferences. Third, managers must evaluate employees' feedback on the appropriateness of TDL.

Management must also "walk the talk" by using advanced technologies to communicate key business information that affects employee learning and performance. This kind of communication is part of a broader process that emphasizes TDL and performance systems that align the efforts of functions, departments, and people. Finally, managers must encourage supervisors to support TDL learning for employees.

Supervisors, TDL implementation needs

The supervisor/learner relationship is a critical link in the learning and performance process, and TDL initiatives require that this link be strengthened. Supervisors must communicate and integrate the relationship between business strategies, CBL needs, and TDL options. They should inform employees of self-paced courseware and distance learning programs, and they should discuss employee expectations before anyone enrolls in technology-based training programs. Finally, supervisors must give employees adequate time during the workday to complete self-paced TDL programs.

Learners' TDL implementation needs

These days, learning and performance is part of the job, which necessitates that employees learn to use TDL options. Not every program will suit every employee, so each individual must explore the potential benefits of each TDL option. Employees are encouraged to identify at what levels and what times they prefer to learn because the menu of TDL options is unlimited, but the individual must take responsibility for implementing a learning strategy.

The Pilot and Launch

Many CBL initiatives fail not because of efforts at linking competency development to business strategies, nor because of failure to develop an effective competency model and learning interventions. They fail because the initiative of launching a successful CBL program never got off the ground.

PILOT PROGRAMS

In simplest terms, a pilot program is a smaller version or trial run of a more extensive launch of a product or service. It is an opportunity to review deficiencies in the program design, implementation mechanisms, learning material or media, or learning assessment process that need to be corrected before the program is fully implemented.

Benefits of a Pilot

If you have used a CBL project team to identify the competency development needs of your organization in a timely fashion, then each CBL program will have its own pilot testing needs. A well-designed pilot will:

1. Assess the impact of the program at the job performance and organizational level. It will answer these questions:

   • Have the employee competencies that most significantly contribute to achieving job outputs been identified?

   • Are program participants acquiring these competencies?

   • Can employees apply the competencies on the job?

   • What are the contributions of the program to the achievement of the organization's strategic goals?

2. Assess behavioral change resulting from the program. Measuring changes in job performance can be heightened by use of a pilot program.

3. Validate the program. The CBL program should improve performance. Testing and validating what it is designed to do before a formal, organization-wide launch is critical.

4. Evaluate reactions to specific cases, exercises, and simulations.

5. Evaluate reactions to the broader program design and competency acquisition process.

6. Provide information about the quality of the program, focusing on issues of program design, development, or administration.

7. Assess management and employees support for the program. Is the readiness for change backed up by the resources (participation, endorsement, application) of the CBL program or intervention?

HOW DOES A PILOT PROGRAM WORK?

There are many approaches to conducting pilot programs. These five basic suggestions are typical.

1. Identify what to test

Remember that CBL programs are results-oriented. The focus should be on identifying and verifying the relationship between the program's design and employee achievement. Second, verify that results-oriented job outputs are linked to business strategies.

You may also want to use the pilot to evaluate reactions to specific cases, exercises, and simulations; the broader program design; the quality of the program; and general logistical support. Remember, however, the bottom line remains: "Does the program do what it is supposed to do?"

2. Select the "right" pilot group

A pilot program is only as effective as the selection and participation of its members. These recommendations help you maximize this success.

- Make sure you have the right group that represents the critical stakeholders and constituencies.

- Make sure that they understand their role in refining and improving the program before the launch.

- Consider pilot group members as the right representatives for the final product. Are they highly motivated and productive employees with peer credibility?

- Members should have the right attitude toward their company, job, and competency-based learning.

- Members should reflect the right power balance. Do they possess both technical knowledge and personal power to influence peers, colleagues, and users about the formal launch of the program?

3. Conduct and respond to the pilot offering

You are now ready to offer the program in conditions closely resembling those of the formal launch. Take advantage of collecting feedback that will be used to hone the program to the sharpest edge.

4. Modify the program according to results

Be prepared to make necessary changes as a result of conducting the pilot program. The following suggestions for change are based on material appearing in *Competency-Based Performance Improvement*. Plan to:

- Clarify estimates of the participants' prerequisite competencies.

- Identify gaps in the meaningfulness or usefulness of the instructional presentation.

- Modify inappropriate expectations of the number of competencies that employees can realistically achieve.

- Improve any learner assessment activities that lack specific directions.

5. Reward pilot participants

Launching the Competency-Based Learning Program

Providing an organization with a competency-based performance improvement solution, one that links business strategies to improving individual performance, is not a casual activity. It is a timely and urgent matter. The CBL is a nonnegotiable option requiring a well-planned, full-scale launch.

Launching a CBL program is relatively accessible if you follow these steps.

1. Establish and sustain momentum.

2. Build on the CBL process.

3. Position the product.

4. Self-market through strategic channels.

5. Keep the administration simple.

Each of these five steps offers unlimited potential. *Establishing and sustaining momentum* (step 1) should be thought of as launching a United Way membership drive. The "thermometer of enrollments" posted in the town square and corporate intranet never begins at "zero." Rather, the first announcement that appears is around 30%. In other words, both United Way memberships campaigns and competency-based learning initiatives "debut" when momentum has already been established.

Building the CBL process (step 2) is relatively easy, for such initiatives are described as self-marketing. In other words, all of the stakeholders are involved in the early planning process. Those individuals, teams, and business units who have helped assess needs now become a fluent channel to both *position the product* (step 3) and *self-market through channels* (step 4). The designer of a CBL initiative is not creating a generalized "one-size-fits-all" training program. Rather, the focus is on a systematic approach to improving performance. The end product, a learning and performance intervention, was launched when front-end need analysis, assessment, and planning responded to strategic business goals.

Finally, *keeping the administration simple* (step 5) is of critical importance. Many of the end-users have suffered from "just-in-case" or "just-by-persisting" training. They have had to jump hurdles of scheduling, registration, travel, and cancellation. The opportunity to select a competency-based learning program must be a user-friendly, customer-driven process. Keep the administration simple by eliminating redundancies of registration, recordkeeping, and evaluation. Virtual learning requires virtual and simple administration.

For More Information

The list below is provided to help you learn more about how others have implemented their competency-based learning programs.

Bassi, Laurie J. and Darlene Russ-Eft (Editors). *What Works: Assessment, Development and Measurement.* Alexandria, VA: American Society for Training and Development, 1997.

Broad, Mary L. (Editor) and Jack J. Phillips. *Transferring Learning to the Workplace* (In Action Series). Alexandria, VA: American Society for Training and Development, 1997.

Broad, Mary L. and John W. Newstrom. *Transfer of Training: Action-Packed Strategies to Ensure High Pay off From Training Investments.* New York: Addison-Wesley Longman, Inc., 1997.

Kirkpatrick, Donald L. *Another Look at Evaluating Training Programs.* Alexandria, VA: American Society for Training and Development, 1998.

Marquardt, Michael J. *Building the Learning Organization.* New York: McGraw-Hill, 1996.

Parry, Scott B. *Evaluating the Impact of Training.* Alexandria, VA: American Society for Training and Development, 1997.

Phillips, Jack J. *Return on Investment in Training and Performance Improvement Programs.* Birmingham, AL: Gulf Publishing Co., 1997.

PART IV

Evaluating and Measuring Competency-Based Learning Programs

EVALUATION AND MEASUREMENT

···

Designing and implementing competency-based learning
programs begins with linking business goals to core organiza-
tional and job competencies. Developing a competency model
focusing on those competencies needed for exemplary perfor-
mance comes next. Finally, a competency curriculum that links
opportunities for performance improvement to an integrated
offering of group and self-directed learning is necessary.
This discussion of designing and implementing CBL
is a good place to start. However, we are not done yet.

···

Competency Development is a Continuous Process

EVALUATE, MEASURE AND START AGAIN

Markets are not static, and any organization wishing to maintain or improve its market position needs to reinvent itself continually. Core competencies must be measured and evaluated to see if they meet the performance improvement needs of individuals and the organization. You may find that new competencies and learning interventions are needed continuously, and thus, you may have to continue the competency development process. The Strategic Learning Systems model appearing on page 5 illustrates that the competency-based performance improvement process continually responds to the requirements of the changing external and organizational environment.

NEW EVALUATION REQUIREMENTS FOR TRAINERS AND ORGANIZATIONS

Many of you are reengineering a traditional training function to meet new corporate needs. This requires you to examine how you evaluate learning and measure performance, and it requires the traditional trainer to assume a critical role as performance consultant.

Review the following inventory, "New Evaluation Mindsets: From Trainer to Performance Consultant," based on material from *Performance Consulting: Moving Beyond Training* by Dana Gaines Robinson and James C. Robinson.

NEW EVALUATION MINDSETS: FROM TRAINER TO PERFORMANCE CONSULTANT

	Traditional Trainers	Performance Consultants
Focus	Identifies and addresses employee training needs	Identifies and addresses employee performance needs
Accountability	Measures number of participant days and courses	Measures the contribution of training and non-training actions for performance and cost benefit
Measurement	Participants evaluate reactions and learning	Measures performance change and cost and learning benefits results
Assessment	Identifies employee training needs	Assesses performance gaps and their reasons
Relationship to Organizational Goals	Training programs have limited linkage to business goals	Training programs have High linkage to organization's goals producing measurable results

Evaluating Results-Oriented CBL Learning Programs

Competency-based learning is self-marketing; that is, it is a win-win process helping individuals and organizations improve performance through continuous learning. Similarly, it is a high-visibility, results-oriented process that is self-evaluating. If we follow the systems approach to competency development, these statements should be true.

A CBL Results-Oriented, Self-Evaluation

The results of our competency-based curriculum and programs are evident because we have:

- Identified employee competencies that most directly contribute to achieving job outputs.
- Assured that employees have acquired these competencies through the design and development of learning opportunities.
- Seen improved job performance as a result of the CBL programs and interventions.
- Achieved organizational goals by linking competency development to business plans.
- Responded to workplace constraints in designing and implementing a CBL program.

Remember, our constant has been bottom-line results. We are no longer evaluating random "training events," but, rather, the results of a competency-based performance improvement system. Competency development has been our strategy of choice for organizational change, and CBL programs and learning interventions have been the driver of the strategy.

Models for Competency-Based Learning Evaluation

Each practitioner brings to the CBL process different needs and expectations, because practitioners range from individuals with entry-level training positions in small companies to senior officers in Fortune 500 organizations.

Four Levels of Training Evaluation and ROI

CBL requires an evaluation process that measures business results attributable to learning and performance initiatives. However, many of us—for many valid reasons—are not there yet. Here is a review of the four levels of training evaluation that appeared in Donald Kirkpartrick's *Evaluating Training Programs*. A select discussion of each level of evaluation will provide you with an opportunity to measure your current level of evaluation and determine your "next step."

While prioritizing results, it is important to recognize the importance of each level and realize that no level should be ignored. Remember that you may be designing, implementing, and evaluating multiple CBL projects concurrently, and each project may be at a different level of performance.

In addition, Jack L. Phillips, writing in *Return on Investment in Training and Performance Improvement Programs*, enhances Kirkpatrick's model by suggesting that return on investment (ROI) calculations are possible not only at Level 4 Results, but on all levels of evaluation. This combined Four Levels of Evaluation and ROI approach is presented as a synergistic framework for competency-based learning evaluation.

The Four Levels of Evaluation

Your review and response to the following self-assessment exercise will help you align the evaluation process and needs of your performance-driven organization. Please identify a current CBL project and assess where you are in the evaluation and corresponding return on investment process.

Level l. Reaction

Evaluation at this level measures how those who participate in the program react to it. This is important for several reasons including: 1. It provides suggestions for improving future programs; 2. It indicates that the trainers need feedback to meet trainee needs; 3. It provides quantitative information to share with program stakeholders; 4. It provides information that can be used to establish performance standards for future programs.

Donald Kirkpatrick presents the following eight recommendations for Level l evaluation:

1. Determine what you want to find out.

2. Design a form that will quantify reactions.

3. Encourage written comments and suggestions.

4. Get 100 percent immediate response.

5. Get honest responses.

6. Develop acceptable standards.

7. Measure reactions against standards, and take appropriate action.

8. Communicate reactions as appropriate.

Level 1 ROI: Beyond the Smile Sheets

Level 1 evaluation is often underestimated and dismissed by some as simply "smile sheets." Jack Phillips suggests that if this level also includes planned application of training, the important data obtained can ultimately be used in return on investment calculations. With this in mind he encourages the use of the following five important questions to ask on Level 1 feedback questionnaires.

Planned Improvement

1. As a result of this program what specific actions will you attempt as you apply what you have learned?

2. Please indicate what specific measures, outcomes, or projects will change as a result of your actions.

3. As a result of the anticipated changes in the above, please estimate (in monetary values) the benefits to your organization over a period of one year.

4. What is the basis of this estimate?

5. What confidence, expressed as a percentage, can you put in your estimate? (0%=No Confidence; 100%=Certainty)

Source: *Return on Investment in Training and Performance Improvement Programs*

Level 2. Learning

This level measures the extent to which participants change attitudes, improve knowledge, and increase skill as a result of attending the program.

Kirkpatrick recommendation:

1. Use a control group, if practical.

2. Evaluate knowledge, skills, and attitudes before and after the program. Use a paper-and-pencil test to measure knowledge and attitudes, and use a performance test to measure skills.

3. Get a 100 percent response.

4. Use the results of the evaluation to take appropriate action.

Level 2 ROI: Testing for Change

Level 2 evaluation provides opportunities for testing for changes in skills and knowledge. And, Jack Phillips writing in *Return on Investment* suggests that "when there is a statistically significant relationship between test scores and on-the-job performance, and the performance can be converted to monetary units, then it is possible to use test scores to estimate the ROI from the program."

He presents the following six steps to support this process:

1. Ensure that the program content reflects desired on-the-job performance.

2. Develop an end-of-program test that reflects program content.

3. Establish a statistical relationship between test data and output performance for participants.

4. Predict performance levels of each participant with given test scores.

5. Convert performance data to monetary value.

6. Compare total predicted value of program with program costs.

7. Consider costs versus benefits.

Level 3. Behavior

Evaluation at this level measures the extent to which change in behavior has occurred because the participants attend the training program. This level of evaluation is obviously more complicated and difficult for several reasons. First, trainees cannot change their behavior until they have an opportunity to do so. Second, it is impossible to predict when a change in behavior will occur. Finally, the rewards for changing behavior will encourage the trainee to apply the learning to the job.

Level 3 ROI: Raising the Bar

Organizations expect participants to change their on-the-job behaviors as the results of the CBL experience. As Jack Phillips suggests an increasingly stronger assumption is being made "for most programs that if the knowledge and skills are applied, then results will follow."

The following six steps, presented in *Return on Investment* are used to measure the valued on-the-job behavior change and calculate the ROI:

1. Develop competencies for the target job.

2. Indicate percentage of job success that is covered in the training program.

3. Determine monetary value of competencies using salaries and employee benefits of participants.

4. Compute the worth of pre- and post-program skill levels.

5. Subtract post-program values from pre-program values.

6. Compare the total added benefits with the program costs.

Level 4. Results

The final results that occurred because the participants attended the program. Historically most training programs have been aimed at accomplishing some worthy results-improved quality, productivity, safety, profits and teamwork. Donald Kirkpatrick provides a list of guidelines helpful for this process.

Donald Kirkpatrick presents the following recommendations for Level 4 evaluation:

1. Use a control group, if practical.

2. Allow time for results to be achieved.

3. Measure before and after the program, if practical.

4. Repeat the measurement at appropriate times.

5. Consider cost versus benefits.

6. Be satisfied with evidence if proof is not possible.

Level 4 ROI: Training vs. Business Results

Increasingly more Level 4 evaluation is focusing on the business results that have been influenced by the learning and performance initiative. These output variables may include cost reduction, productivity increases, improved quality, reduced response time and most importantly increased customer service.

Jack Phillips has identified two critical issues involved in Level 4 ROI development.

1. Isolate the Effects of Training

When a program has been conducted and the output variables have changed, the first step for the evaluator is to determine the extent to which the training program changed the output variable. Other factors, improved economic conditions, change in workforce; new processes may also impact on the improved results.

2. Convert Business Results to a Monetary Unit

Critical to the successful use of this level of evaluation is the conversion of output data reduction in error rates, decrease in response times, improved customer services to actual monetary units and value. And as the closing section of this chapter indicates, not only is it important to calculate the ROI on tangibles, but there remains the challenge of evaluating and valuing the intangibles.

A Final Note on Model One

Completion of this inventory accomplishes two purposes. First, it presents Donald Kirkpatrick's *Four Levels of Evaluation* as a critical building block for the CBL evaluation process. Second, it presents Jack Phillips' research on *Return on Investment* as a synergistic partner in the evaluation process. Clearly, ROI calculations can be developed at all four levels of evaluation. While traditionally most practitioners have focused only on level 3 and 4 for ROI calculations, levels 1 and 2 estimates can also be a useful tool for managers, practitioners and CBL participants. All learning and performance stakeholders must gain a better understanding of the economic impact of training through a collaborative effort of evaluating the four levels of training programs and the return on investment. Competency-based learning continues to serve as the cornerstone of this process.

This informal inventory has accomplished another purpose, it presented an integrated four-step process of evaluating training programs and return on investment. Completion of this inventory also provides you with a rich application exercise. Afterwards, you should be able to answer several critical questions. Are your CBL programs simply measuring trainee's reactions, or do participants learn the material? Has the evaluation process checked for behavior changes back on the job? And, finally, can you calculate business results in monetary terms attributable to learning?

Model Two: The Dubois Model

The model described earlier in Part I, developed by David R. Dubois, measures the responsiveness of the performance improvement system for the employee's job performance needs and the strategic needs of the organization.

Evaluating Intangibles

Evaluation is a most important element of any learning and performance initiative. Clearly, efforts that focus on core competencies and use of learning as a strategic source of competitive advantage all reinforce the need for improved, accurate, and continuous evaluation.

Recognize the complexity of evaluating training

However, there has always been—and will probably continue to be—difficulty in isolating and evaluating training's effect from other performance improvement interventions. The use of alternative delivery technologies and electronic learning will further complicate issues of measurement.

Writing in *Tracking Operational Results*, Dana Gaines Robinson and James C. Robinson encourage the use of "shadow pricing" as an alternative to traditional measurement. Essentially this practice encourages the learning and performance professional to invent a value or measurement when no convenient hard measurement for training benefits exists. Examples may include time savings, increased productivity, and improved industry standards.

Value the Intangibles

Remember two things. First, as a learning and performance professional, identify practical guidelines for tracking operational returns by calculating both the costs and benefits of training. Second, appreciate and value the intangibles.

In simplest terms, intangible benefits include any activities, qualities, or conditions that have value, but are difficult to quantify, since not all learning and performance results can be reported in bottom-line hard numbers. As Anthony Carnevale and Eric Schulze write in *Return on Investment: Accounting for Training,* "Decision makers should consider the potential risk of not investing in them and should estimate how substantial intangible benefits might possible be."

Assume responsibility and leadership for improving the evaluation process

Leadership for improving evaluation approaches is coming from several fronts, including the American Society for Training and Development. The ASTD Performance Metrics Working Group has constructed as a guiding principle: "Our purpose is to use measurement as a means to promote continuous improvement in the cost and performance effectiveness of learning." Each of us must assume responsibility and leadership for improving the evaluation process.

Benchmarking and Metrics

The process of benchmarking and the concept of metrics have emerged as complimentary strategies for evaluating CBL programs. Benchmarking is the process of comparing one organization's practices with another. By so doing, you identify your organization's strengths and weaknesses and help your organization improve its processes by learning how other organizations do it better. Metrics focus on measurements of performance. Metrics provide the learning organization with tools to measure learning and performance activities, results and efficiency.

Benchmarking can be applied to any businesses, as long as their core functions are similar. Use it in the following step-by-step exercise.

BENCHMARKING STEP-BY-STEP

Step 1. Decide on what to benchmark. What are your organization's benchmarking needs? What factors are most critical to learning and performance and how will you measure them?

Your example:

Step 2. Identify benchmarking partners. Partnering with internal and external organizations can help you identify best practices. In particular, suppliers can help you meet your benchmarking objectives.

Your example:

Step 3. Gathering information. Your efforts at determining what and how to measure CBL can be enhanced through information provided by other organizations. For example, a series of metrics have been developed by the ASTD.

Your example:

Step 4. Analyze. Identify the performance gap that exists within your organization and that of the "best" demonstrated practice.

Your example:

Step 5. Implement for effectiveness. Consider the implications of the results. Find the best strategy to report the results to the people it affects and the identification of opportunities for improvement.

Your example:

Conclusion

Your efforts of reading this book will soon be rewarded. It is the assumption of the author and publisher that you have mastered the basics of designing and implementing a competency-based learning program. We assume that you not only have developed a basic understanding of a competency vocabulary, but that you can apply competency concepts to meeting the changing needs of adult learners and their learning organizations.

As you build your very own foundation for competency-based learning programs you learn to appreciate the value of using a strategic learning systems approach. You also have the ability to make the decision of whether to design your very own competency model or customize models designed by others. Once this model is in place you will have the specific resources to design an integrated competency-based curriculum that meets the needs of your organization. The opportunity to accelerate this process is also within reach if you chose to partner with a supplier to design a curriculum and also make use of off-the-shelf training materials.

In addition, you should now have a competitive advantage in implementing a successful CBL Program. You are now in the position to make use of both project team and communication strategies to roll out both program pilot and launch. In addition, you have a competitive advantage in making use of specific guidelines for implementing the CBL program that actively involves a collaborative partnership between learner, supervisor, and manager. Perhaps of greatest importance, you now understand the importance of providing self-directed professionals with opportunities for various self-directed delivery options.

Finally, you can now make use of a results-oriented evaluation process that places efforts on achieving a return on investment. You have been encouraged to go beyond the smile sheets, test for change in on-the-job performance, and isolate the effects of training on business results. Most importantly, you are out of the "business of training" and into the "business of learning and performance." Congratulations on your efforts to date and successes yet to come.

Appendix

Bibliography

Available Directly Through Crisp Publications

Shandler, Donald. *Reengineering the Training Function: How to Align Training with the New Corporate Agenda.* 1996, 300 pages, hard cover, $39.95.

Shandler, Donald and Susan E. Kruppenbach. *The Training Operations Reengineering Survey.* 60 question items, 1996, $6.95.

Shandler, Donald and Susan E. Kruppenbach. *The Training Operations Reengineering Survey Facilitator's Guide.* 1996, St Lucie Press, $24.95.

Steinbach, Robert. *Successful Lifelong Learning,* 1999, Crisp Publications, Menlo Park, CA, $10.95.

Crisp Editors, *Extending the Corporate University,* Crisp Publications, Menlo Park, CA: 1997.

Articles

Parry, Scott B. "The Quest for Competencies." *Training,* July, 1996.

Carnevale, Anthony, and Eric Schultz. "Return on Investment: Accounting for Training," *Training & Development Journal,* Vol. 44, No. 7 (July 1990).

Booklet

Robinson, Dana Gaines and James C. Robinson, "Tracking Operational Results," *Info-Line,* Issue 9112, (December 1991).

Books

Boulter, Nick, Murry Daiziel, and Jackie Hill (Eds.). *People and Competencies: The Route to Competitive Advantage.* London: Hay/McBer, Kogan Page, 1992.

Boyatzis, Richard E. *The Competent Manager: A Model for Effective Performance.* New York: John Wiley & Sons, Inc., 1982.

Carnevale, Anthony Patrick. *American and the New Economy: How New Competitive Standards Are Radically Changing American Workplaces.* San Francisco: Jossey-Bass Publishers, 1991.

Competency-Based Education (Volume 8): Professional Development Series. Stillwater, OK: Mid-America Vocational Curriculum Consortium, Inc: 1992.

Craig, Ed. Robert L. *The ASTD Training & Development Handbook: A Guide to Human Resource Development.* New York: McGraw-Hill, 1996.

Dubois, David. *The Executive's Guide to Competency-Based Performance Improvement:* Amherst, MA: Human Resource Development Press, 1997.

Dubois, David D. *Competency-Based Performance Improvement: A Strategy for Organizational Change.* Amherst, MA: Human Resource Development Press, 1993.

Kirkpatrick, Donald. *Evaluating Training Programs: The Four Levels.* San Francisco: Berrett-Koehler Publishers, 1994.

Knowles, Malcom S. *The Adult Learner: A Neglected Species.* Np, Ny.

Knowles, Malcom S. *The ASTD Training & Development Handbook.* Np, Ny.

Marquardt, Michael J. *Building the Learning Organization.* New York: McGraw-Hill, 1996.

Maul, June Paradise and Joel D. Krauss, "Outsourcing in Training and Education." *The ASTD Training & Development Handbook: A Guide to Human Resource Development.* Robert L. Craig, Ed. New York: McGraw-Hill, 1996.

McLagan, Patricia and Christo Nel. *The Age of Participation.* San Francisco: Berrett-Koehler, 1997.

Meister, Jeanne C. *Corporate Quality Universities: Lessons in Building a World-Class Work Force.* Alexandria, VA: American Society for Training and Development, 1993.

Robinson, Dana Gaines and James C. Robinson. *Performance Consulting: Moving Beyond Training.* San Francisco: Berrett-Koehler, 1996.

Rothwell, William J. *Beyond Training and Development: State-of-the-Art Strategies for Enhancing Human Performance.* AMACOM, 1996.

Rothwell, William J. and Henry J. Sredl. *The ASTD Reference Guide to Professional Human Resource Development Roles and Competencies.* Amherst, MA: Human Resource Development Press, 1992.

Senge, Peter M. *The Fifth Discipline: The Art and Practice of the Learning Organization.* New York: Doubleday, 1994.

Spencer, Lyle. *Competence at Work: Models for Superior Performance.* NY: John Wiley & Sons, 1993.

Ulrich, David. *Human Resource Champions.* Cambridge: Harvard Business School Press, 1997.

National Retail Skill Standards

Provide Personalized Customer Service

Initiate Customer Contact

- Determine customer's needs by listening and asking questions
- Make shopping experience enjoyable for customer
- Give customer an appropriate greeting
- Inform customer of additional services
- Refer customer to another department or store

Build Customer Relations

- Follow through on commitments made to customer
- Respond to personal needs of shoppers
- Honor manufacturers' warranties
- Adhere to company's return policy
- Handle customer complaints
- Balance responsive phone service with in-store service
- Maintain key information on customers
- Conduct customer follow-up
- Provide customer with personalized business card
- Complete special orders
- Schedule personal appointment with shopper
- Select merchandise in advance

Sell and Promote Products

Determine Customer Needs

- Listen and ask open-ended questions
- Acquire and apply product knowledge
- Request product feedback from customer

- Handle customer objections
- Verify product is appropriate for customer
- Offer alternative sales options

Build the Sale

- Motivate customer to return for future purchases
- Sell customer additional or related merchandise
- Review current advertising and promotions
- Test products to be displayed
- Handle customer returns; transform into new sale
- Initiate/create special promotions
- Convert phone calls into sales
- Encourage customer to open credit accounts and purchase gift certificates

Close the Sale

- Assist customer in making purchase decision
- Handle transaction and related paperwork
- Inform customer of exchange/return policy
- Open, maintain, and close cash register
- Package merchandise appropriately
- Assure that shipping/mailing/deliveries are handled properly

Monitor Inventory

Take Inventory

- Check in merchandise against paperwork
- Assure accurate pricing on merchandise
- Review stock and restock as necessary
- Locate merchandise through inventory system
- Participate in periodic inventory process

Transfer Inventory

- Prepare returned merchandise for resale
- Return inventory to manufacturer/vendor
- Initiate and/or respond to requests for merchandise transfer
- Identify damaged items and handle appropriately
- Initiate repair order

Maintain Appearance of Department/Store

Maintain Stock, Selling and Customer Services Area

- Organize and maintain supplies
- Organize stockroom and storage areas
- Clean selling areas and customer service areas
- Report need for repairs or replacement

Maintain Product Presentation and Displays

- Arrange merchandise
- Relay feedback from customers on the effectiveness of displays
- Maintain displays following company guidelines
- Dismantle displays

Protect Company Assets

Identify and Prevent Loss

- Alert customer to your presence
- Attach and remove security devices
- Account for items after customers use of dressing rooms
- Report stock shrinkage
- Report security violations
- Monitor floor merchandise
- Alert sales associates to suspicious customers

Follow Safety Precautions

- Report safety problems in the department/store
- Follow emergency procedures
- Maintain accurate records

Work as Part of a Department/Store Team
Support Co-Workers

- Share ideas and information about selling, marketing, and products
- Attend store meetings and major events
- Assist or turn over sale to co-worker
- Assist with training and orientation of new employees
- Work out scheduling conflicts with co-workers

Create Competitive Advantage

- Research the competition (products, prices, services)
- Provide manager and peers with feedback on competition
- Track sales versus established standards
- Develop personal and professional goals

For a complete listing of tasks for each skill or more information about the development process, contact the National Retail Federation at (202) 783-7971.

About The Author

Donald Shandler, Ph.D., is Director of Continuing Education, Graduate School, United States Department of Agriculture, where he manages evening and weekend programs, correspondence and online classes, conferences and institutes, and the registrar and bookstore. He is also the chairperson of the Competency-Based Training Task Force, which has been charged with improving service, quality, and learning. He also leads a school-wide market research project for new and responsive learning and performance programs.

Dr. Shandler has served as Director of Education for the National Association of Home Builders, Assistant Vice Chancellor at the University of Maryland University College, and Director of Continuing Education for Southern Illinois University at Edwardsville. He has taught at Boston College, the University of Maryland, and Johns Hopkins University. He is founder of Organizational Development and Research Associates, Inc., a consulting firm.

Other books by Donald Shandler include *From Technical Specialist to Supervisor,* Crisp Publications (1993), *Reengineering the Training Function: How to Align Training with the New Corporate Agenda,* St. Lucie Press (1996), and *Management and Development of the Contingency Workforce: Shaping Strategies for the 21st Century,* St. Lucie Press (to be published in 2000).

Dr. Shandler can be reached at:

Donald Shandler, Ph.D.
Director of Continuing Education
Graduate School, USDA
S. Agriculture Building, Room 1107
1400 Independence Avenue SW
Washington, DC 20250-9901
Voice: (202) 314-3665 Fax: (202) 863-3907
E-mail: donald_shandler@grad.usda.gov